IMAGES
of America

EAST MEADOW

This iconic East Meadow photograph shows a hunting party in front of the Andrew Hoeffner Hotel, which was located on the southwest corner of Prospect and Newbridge (now East Meadow) Avenues. The property, now occupied by Veterans Memorial Park, was purchased by the Hoeffner family in 1914. Fox and rabbit hunting were popular sports at the time, and many of East Meadow's residents participated. The hotel stood at an important central point in East Meadow, and the building is now on display at the Old Bethpage Village Restoration. Proprietor Andrew P. Hoeffner is pictured at far right. (Courtesy Hoeffner family.)

ON THE COVER: This 1940 photograph shows Frances Weiner (back cover), Ernie Hatzelman, and Gretel Zimmerman riding their tricycles down Elmore Avenue in East Meadow. The homes were built during the period of slow suburban growth between the two world wars, when East Meadow still had dirt streets and few trees. (Courtesy Frances Weiner-Mouton.)

IMAGES
of America

EAST MEADOW

Scott M. Eckers

ARCADIA
PUBLISHING

Published by Arcadia Publishing
Charleston, South Carolina

Printed in the United States of America

Library of Congress Control Number: 2022941318

For all general information, please contact Arcadia Publishing:
Telephone 843-853-2070
Fax 843-853-0044
E-mail sales@arcadiapublishing.com
For customer service and orders:
Toll-Free 1-888-313-2665

Visit us on the Internet at www.arcadiapublishing.com

This book is dedicated to the students of East Meadow. May you always be inspired to learn about the past and preserve our community's history.

CONTENTS

ACKNOWLEDGMENTS

This project would not have come to fruition without the help of many individuals who share a love for East Meadow and its history. The assistance of Raymond A. Hoeffner Jr. cannot be overstated. His multigenerational connection to East Meadow proved to be an invaluable source of information and family photographs. The leads Dr. Hoeffner provided to longtime East Meadow families were important links to not only images but also stories and anecdotes that helped frame the entire work. His involvement was truly inspiring.

There are several individuals who were kind enough to provide images and information and who are deserving of thanks: Patrick Pizzo, Timothy Voels, Greg Bottari, and Stephanie Ploski of the East Meadow Union Free School District (UFSD); Susan Marks of Wenwood Oaks; and Jeff Kraut, Jay Zinger, Art Huenke, Brian O'Flaherty, and Eric Poliak. Iris Levin of the county archives helped acquire rare photographs dating back to 1865. Several photographs came from the Steve Buczak collection, a repository of local clippings. Thank you to librarians Ann Glorioso of Levittown and Steve Rung of Hempstead and to East Meadow Public Library director of public relations Jude Schanzer.

Thanks to Howard Kroplick, town historian of North Hempstead, for encouraging local history enthusiasts through his website and books and for providing images and information for this work. Gary Hammond spent a considerable amount of time discussing this project and sharing pictures. Art Kleiner is owed a great thank-you for meeting with me and sharing his collection of original postcards. Sharon Houghey O'Gara met with me to open up her family's collection of photographs to the greater community. William Katz, longtime East Meadow educator, provided many photographs and stories. Carey Welt and John Katalo of the East Meadow Fire Department were both generous in giving of their time to research and provide images.

I wish to thank the Oberle family for meeting with me on several occasions to share their three generations of family and business photographs and for allowing me to conduct interviews about East Meadow's earlier days. Marge Reimels Divan provided oral and written information and original photographs of her family history. Walter Lowden shared his family's history.

Finally, I would like to thank my parents, Linda and Allen, for always inspiring me to learn and teach. Special thanks to my wife and fellow history teacher, Jenny, whose patience and kindness were essential to the research and development of this work.

INTRODUCTION

East Meadow, Long Island, is certainly an active community, and it has been for hundreds of years. Its status as an unincorporated hamlet, however, complicates its identity. It has no local government. So, then, what is East Meadow? This is not a simple question to answer. In doing so, one must examine what constitutes the community, not only according to government designations, but also what is in the hearts and minds of the people who have lived there.

East Meadow is located within the town of Hempstead, formed in 1644. Before the arrival of the Europeans, the earliest residents of the Hempstead Plains were tribes of Algonquian Indians. The name "Merrick" (also Meroke, Merioke, or Mericock) stems from a reference to the plains themselves. In the Massachusetts language, the term means "bare land." In November 1643, the land was sold to Englishmen John Carman and Robert Fordham by members of the local Massapequa, Merrick, and Rockaway tribes. Carman and Fordham had arrived in the Dutch colony from Connecticut with permission from Dutch director general William Kieft.

As an English colony, Hempstead was part of Queens County, one of the original counties of New York. The name means "Town-Spot," suggesting its central importance. Curiously, Town-Spot was also the first name of the Hempstead Common School. The east meadow of the Hempstead village was convenient for grazing, and town residents held the area as common land for their cattle. The earliest recorded use of the name "East Meadow" appeared in town records in 1658, authorizing William Jacocks and Edward Raynor to keep cows there from approximately April to October.

During the American Revolution, the British held New York City and much of Long Island for the entire war. The loyalties of local residents were divided. Those residing in the southern parts of Hempstead were generally Loyalists, supporting the British crown; those residing in the northern parts of the town were generally Patriots, supporting independence. This rift was so significant that the town split after the war ended. In 1784, North Hempstead Town came into being. South Hempstead would still be known as Hempstead.

Throughout the 19th century, growth was small but steady. Hempstead became the most populous town in Queens County during the antebellum period, with approximately 10,000 residents. New York City was enlarged in 1898 and included the western sections of Queens. The towns of Hempstead, North Hempstead, and Oyster Bay formed the new Nassau County in 1899. At that time, Hempstead had more than 23,000 people. Early suburban development brought quick growth after World War I, but real changes occurred after the Second World War, when baby boom families came in droves from New York City. These new residents completely changed the face of East Meadow from a rural farming community to one of cookie-cutter suburban sprawl. Today, East Meadow is a large contributor to the fact that the town of Hempstead is the largest by population in the United States, with more than 750,000 residents. Although its modern homes are similar in form, the people who live in East Meadow give it a local identity vastly different from neighboring communities.

The first and most significant municipal identity was established during the War of 1812 when a system of common schools was formed in the town. From this original division, East Meadow came into being as a community with actual borders—District No. 3. Since future municipal districts did not follow the same borders, the school district boundary is the only logical way to define East Meadow. For more than 200 years, this designation has bound together the collection of farms and later housing developments that came to be known as East Meadow. The post office further complicated East Meadow's identity problem. For generations, mail was delivered to most of East Meadow through the Hempstead post office, and the hamlet was intrinsically linked to that village. East Meadow's branch opened in 1951, and the designation of ZIP codes followed in 1963. Neither one of these events helped to define East Meadow, as post offices from Levittown and Westbury served portions of the school district's boundaries, confusing postal customers. East Meadow residents could not even convince the telephone company to designate a common exchange name for the hamlet, even after threatening to boycott the service for a month in 1952.

East Meadowites have seen great success in the arts, sports, literature, and politics—but these individuals do not define East Meadow. Suburban commuters replaced farmers, but neither experience can completely define what it means to live there. Great moments in automobile racing and airplane feats have taken place in or over the community, but those do not define East Meadow. Notable crimes have taken place, and those certainly do not define East Meadow—nor do they warrant space in this book. Only the collective memory and shared experiences of the people who have called it home can define what makes East Meadow such a warm and inviting place to raise a family or conduct business.

Neighborhood children dance in a local elementary school gymnasium. (Courtesy East Meadow Jewish Center.)

One

MAKING A LIVING
ON THE PLAINS

The Hoeffner children—from left to right, Ralph, Matilda, Edward (rear), Clifford, Helen, and Andrew Jr.—pose with their goat in this c. 1919 photograph. For many children growing up in East Meadow, helping on the farm was not just a fun pastime—it was vital to the family's success. This remained true for farm children until the development boom. In 1942, the East Meadow Common School District successfully petitioned the state to open a week later than usual due to the number of older students needed to help on area farms. (Courtesy Hoeffner family.)

The Carman-Lowden homestead stood on the north side of Hempstead (Bethpage) Turnpike. It was home to one of East Meadow's oldest and most prominent farming and civic families, the members of which worked the land for well over 150 years. The homestead (pictured here in 1915 and 1984) was the only inn for travelers on the turnpike between Hempstead and Farmingdale. A tollhouse stood near the intersection with Carman Avenue. The Lowdens became founding members in the establishment of the East Meadow Republican Club and members of the board of education. Walter Lowden Jr. recalls hearing that his father was the first person to deliver the mail, using his motorcycle, when the Rural Route to East Meadow was set up from the Hempstead Post Office. Yearly spectators of the Vanderbilt Cup Races would come from New York City and rent rooms in the house. The homestead was demolished in 1985 and sold for commercial development. (Both, courtesy Nassau County Archives.)

The Carman family can trace its Town of Hempstead heritage back to Benjamin Carman (1688–1735) and Ann Mott (b. 1681). Records of the Carman family living in East Meadow begin with James Raynor Carman (1779–1858). Prominent members of the Carman-Lowden family are pictured above. At left is Charles Pine Carman (1834–1913) and at right is his sister Mary Ann Carman Lowden (1844–1921), who married Richard Lowden (1841–1913). The last resident of the Carman-Lowden homestead was Mary E. Lowden (1924–2011), an art teacher in Hempstead. The Carman-Lowden homestead is shown below in an 1887 painting by R. Bond. (All, courtesy Carman-Lowden family.)

Richard Lowden (1841–1913) married Mary Ann Carman in 1867. He was a trustee of the East Meadow Methodist Church. An amusing newspaper article from 1900 tells the story of Lowden getting into a dispute with a traveling minister, the Reverend Ross Taylor of Manhattan. Taylor, a lifelong friend of Lowden, sent his favorite horse to board on the East Meadow pastures after it was run down. When Taylor visited the church to conduct services and found his horse was healthier than expected, he asked Lowden to return the horse to him in New York City. Lowden refused to release the horse until Taylor paid $192 in boarding fees. (Courtesy Carman-Lowden family.)

Several generations of the Fish family lived on the northwest corner of North Jerusalem Road and Newbridge (now East Meadow) Avenue. The original farmhouse stood for more than 100 years close to a pond that once existed near the current-day shopping plaza. The Fish family raised livestock and grew peaches and apples in their orchards. George S. Fish (1859–1946) was a civic leader and served on the school board for many years. His house, seen here, was eventually moved to the south side of North Jerusalem Road when the land was sold for the Central Homes development after World War II. Just down the street, on the northeast corner of North Jerusalem Road and Bellmore Avenue (then known as Westbury Road), stood the Seaman homestead. The Seaman family was very prominent in the Wantagh (Jerusalem) community, southeast of East Meadow. (Courtesy Hoeffner family.)

The Noon Inn at Prospect and Newbridge (now East Meadow) Avenues was one of the most popular meeting sites in East Meadow. It was built around 1836 by Sylvanus Bedell and subsequently owned by different families, most notably John H. and Mary Noon, who operated the inn between 1848 and 1861. John Noon became a wealthy real estate investor in the area. After operation by the Seaman and Glinsmann families, the property was sold to Heinrich (Henry) and Lena Schultze in 1883. Above, members of the Wisdom, Fasnacht, Mangan, Ulsman, Gass, Fance, and Schultze families are pictured outside the inn around 1900. Below, Henry Schultze is shown at work in his bar at Schultze's Hotel around 1890. (Both, courtesy Nassau County Archives.)

Above, the Schultze Hotel is pictured around 1900. Heinrich Schultze sold the property to Andrew and Elizabeth Hoeffner in January 1914. The Hoeffners moved from Fosters Meadow, a German farming community near Elmont, and took over operations of the East Meadow Hotel, selling Welz & Zerweck beer until Prohibition. The Hoeffners returned to farming while raising their seven boys and two girls in the historic house. East Meadow farmers, including the Hoeffners, were mostly market or truck farmers, regularly taking their goods by mule, horse, and later motor vehicle to the Wallabout Market (now Brooklyn Navy Yard) in order to sell to customers in New York City. Below, Andrew P. Hoeffner Sr. works on his fields with a potato grader around 1915. He farmed from 8 to 150 acres during his time as a farmer and rented part of the Barnum property before development claimed much of the farmland. (Above, courtesy Nassau County Archives; below, courtesy Hoeffner family.)

Above, Andrew P. Hoeffner and his wife, Elizabeth, are pictured with their first four children—from left to right, Matilda, Helen, Andrew Jr., and Edward—on the steps of the East Meadow Hotel around 1912. Below, John Schlick, brother of Elizabeth Schlick Hoeffner, poses on his motorcycle. The c. 1915 photograph was taken looking south down current-day East Meadow Avenue from the intersection of Prospect Avenue. In the background, the 1868 one-room schoolhouse is visible. It was moved from Front Street to the Schultze property, just south of the current post office, by a team of horses. The old schoolhouse became the East Meadow Hall, used for social and political functions and strongly connected to the Methodist Episcopal Church across the street. East Meadow Hall was destroyed in the early 1960s; its original school bell was salvaged. At left is the Moskowski homestead. (Courtesy Hoeffner family.)

Transportation on the swampy, brushy plains was difficult before the modern era, and farm families depended on horses and mules. The automobile was prominently featured in many early-20th-century photographs of East Meadow. Above, Andrew and Elizabeth Hoeffner and their children are shown in 1920 with their Model T, the second car in East Meadow. This photograph was taken at the corner of Haycarter's Lane (Prospect Avenue) and Newbridge (East Meadow) Avenue at the East Meadow Hotel. Haycarter's was named as such because it was the winding road to the hay fields. Below, Edward A. Hoeffner stands outside his car in the 1930s, with Raymond A. Hoeffner inside. The Steck House can be seen in the background, later the site of Meadow Dairy. (Courtesy Hoeffner family.)

In the Prohibition years, running the old inn was no longer profitable, and the Hoeffner family turned back to farming and eventually construction. By 1951, the ACE Hoeffner Construction Company had been formed, and the property was used to store construction materials for local projects. The family built the East Meadow Post Office on the southern edge of their property and leased the land to the federal government. Previously, Rural Free Delivery would deliver the mail from Hempstead and Hicksville. Above, the ACE Hoeffner Construction Company is seen with the former Noon Inn starting to fall into disrepair. The Town of Hempstead took the land by eminent domain in 1963, and Hoeffner's Corner is within Veterans Memorial Park today. The building was moved to the Old Bethpage Village Restoration, where it serves root beer to many school children as the Noon Inn. Nearby, the Alsheimer family farmed the land on property that became East Meadow Bowl. (Above, courtesy Hoeffner family; below, courtesy Alsheimer family.)

The Otto Muller Florist was established in 1927 on what became the PathMark property between Hempstead Turnpike and Front Street. Kurt Weiss worked for Otto Muller and subsequently married his daughter Lena in 1934. Together, Muller and Weiss purchased additional parcels of land, expanding the business to 23 acres. Weiss established Kurt Weiss Florist in 1960 as a second-generation owner and built a house on the property, seen above in the 1960s. Kurt's son Russell took over the business and moved it to Center Moriches. Today, it is the largest distributor of poinsettias on the East Coast. The greenhouse property was sold for commercial development. Below, azaleas are grown at the nursery. (Both, courtesy Lenora Weiss White.)

Emil Oberle Sr. came to East Meadow in 1924 and erected greenhouses on eight acres of land at the corner of Newbridge (now East Meadow) Avenue and North Jerusalem Road. Joan Swedberg's family arrived in East Meadow from Phoenix in 1936 and settled on Stuyvesant Avenue. The two were grade school sweethearts at Newbridge Road School. After eighth grade, the students boarded a bus from Sabia's Corner (at the intersection of North Jerusalem and Newbridge Roads) to Hempstead High School. They married soon after graduation. According to Joan, that section of the hamlet was "a few houses but primarily woods" but "a nice place to grow up." Pictured below are Emil, Joan, and Alana Oberle. (Both, courtesy Oberle family.)

Families walked through the old graveyard to get to Sunday school at the old Methodist church, and the teenagers would hang out at Mr. and Mrs. Pollack's candy store near Kenmore Street and Newbridge Road. Mr. Fish, who owned a peach orchard and farm across the street, would show Emil different farming technology even though the locals plowed with horses. The Oberles operated the greenhouses (seen below in 1976) and florist shop for three generations, until selling the land for development in 2016. Above, the Oberle children run a tomato stand in 1968. (Both, courtesy Oberle family.)

The oldest established house of worship in East Meadow is the Methodist Episcopal Church, seen in the 1910 photograph at right. After many years of itinerant preachers, the church was organized by Peter Lewis, David Sprague, John S. Smith, Joseph Smith, and Parmonus Post in 1857. A year later, John and Mary Noon, who owned the East Meadow Hotel, donated property on the eastern side of Newbridge (East Meadow) Avenue for the purpose of building a church. The original wooden frame structure was replaced in 1897; the building still stands. A cemetery behind the church contains the remains of some of East Meadow's earliest settlers. Several church members interred in the graveyard were born in the 18th century. The Rowehl family's retirement home, seen below around 1936, was moved to Hempstead Turnpike and became Dalton's Funeral Home. (Right, courtesy Gary Hammond; below, courtesy Margaret Reimels Divan.)

One of the more prominent and stable farming establishments on the east side of the hamlet was the Rowehl family's 219 acres south of Hempstead Turnpike. Diedrich Gerhard Rowehl purchased this land from Theodore and Pauline Pietycker in 1854, and it became a community of four generations of his 48 descendants in nine farmhouses. The brush, grass, and wildflowers of the plains were cleared for farmland and grazing. Eventually, the family cultivated potatoes and sold hay to Cooper's Field in Hempstead. This is the original homestead at 177 Bellmore Road. (Courtesy Margaret Reimels Divan.)

The original 219-acre Rowehl homestead on Bellmore Road was divided into three lots, then into six sections. The property extended into Island Trees and Jerusalem (the southern section of current-day Levittown) and was bisected with the construction of the Wantagh State Parkway in the 1930s. All nine houses still stand, albeit modified, remarkably surviving suburban development

The Rowehl and Granz families started a nursery on their property with large greenhouses, barns, and even a windmill. Orchards surrounded the buildings. Like so many other East Meadow farmers, vegetables produced on the farm were taken by horse, sometimes up to nine hours, to Wallabout Market for sale to New York City. This photograph taken at 176 Bellmore Road shows John, Sis, and Buster Reimels in 1940, the year bathrooms were installed in the house. The outhouse can be seen on the right. (Courtesy Margaret Reimels Divan.)

of the 1950s. The German family names of the postwar streets built on the former Rowehl farm are a testament to the family's influence on East Meadow. Charles D. Rowehl's house at 294 Bellmore Road is now home to the American Legion, which was active in the 1930s as the Christian Wolf Post No. 1082, seen in this 1937 photograph at a social outing. (Courtesy Hoeffner family.)

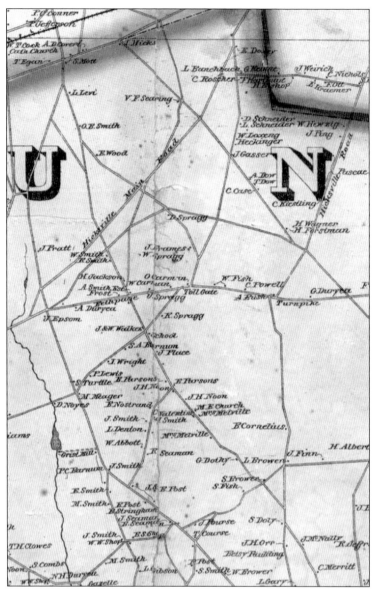

This 1859 map shows the location of many of the families discussed in this chapter. Most of the earliest farm families were descendants of English colonial settlers—some of whom crossed Long Island Sound from Connecticut to form Hempstead Town in 1643. Many of these roads still exist, particularly in the southern section of East Meadow. Note the tollgate on the (Hempstead) Bethpage Turnpike on the south end of the Carman property. The turnpike itself was built from old Indian trails and incorporated as a paid road in 1812. The owners included East Meadow names: Samuel Carman, Joseph Pettit, Abraham Bell, and Laurence Seaman. In 1852, it was sold to the Hempstead and Jamaica Plank Road Company, which laid wooden planks for better travel. This company operated the turnpike for 30 years before the county acquired it. Another influential English family was that of Peter Crosby Barnum, who would become the largest landowner in Queens County. His homes and gristmill can be seen on the west side of Whale Neck Road (Merrick Avenue). J.H. Noon's property lay next to the M.E. Church. (Courtesy Library of Congress.)

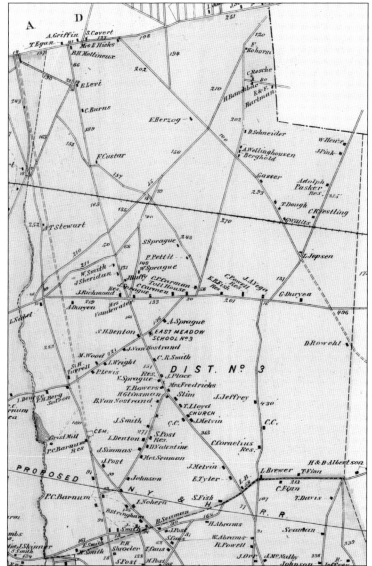

Many main roads had been established by the mid-19th century: Hempstead (Bethpage) Turnpike, Front Street, Whale Neck Road (then Barnum Avenue, now Merrick Avenue), and Westbury Road (now Bellmore Avenue). In 1755, Newbridge Avenue (now East Meadow) was established from the Quaker meetinghouse on Old Country Road in Westbury southeast to Jerusalem (it was severed around 1940). North (Old) Jerusalem Road, established in 1750, was the only east-west road in the southern part of East Meadow. It was eventually straightened; the old section is now called Ennabrock Road. A new Jerusalem Avenue was commissioned south of the old road in 1866. The point where they meet was known as the "Lower Going Over" because early settlers would be "going over" the Meadow Brook. With livestock outnumbering humans, the early roads were built for the easy transportation of animals and were wide enough to accommodate the movement of significant numbers of "cattle and other creatures," in the words of the Town of Hempstead records. This 1873 Beers map shows additional farm families, such as Rowehl and Berg, as well as plans for the straightening of Merrick Avenue, the creation of Bellmore Road, and an extension of a railroad line, which never came to fruition. Note the cemetery on Merrick Avenue. (Courtesy David Rumsey Historical Map Collection.)

Farming was a way of life in East Meadow through the early decades of the 20th century, and local families worked the land alongside summer vacationers from New York City. Dmytro and Anna Kostynick owned a farm at Prospect and Maple Avenues and raised six children there. Above, "Kostynick's Herd" hangs out with the wash (the cows were Molly and Olga). After the Kostynick family built a home on Green Avenue, single women recruited as schoolteachers from colleges by the district superintendent would rent rooms upstairs from 1951 to 1962. Below, Mary Buczak picks crops. Irrigation systems and greenhouses were a common sight on Long Island farms. Until 1950, water for homes came from hand pumps and individual wells. The Pryzmont, Novak, and Wetterich families ran dairies, and their children delivered the milk to customers while riding their bicycles to school. (Above, courtesy Kostynick family; below, courtesy Buczak family.)

Two

LIFESTYLES OF THE RICH AND FAMOUS

People who have lived in East Meadow their entire lives are often surprised to hear that wealthy and famous socialites graced this part of Hempstead Town. In the late 19th and early 20th centuries, names such as Roosevelt, Brisbane, and Vanderbilt were well known in East Meadow. Alva Vanderbilt Belmont built this grand estate called Brookholt on an 800-acre site on Front Street, west of Merrick Avenue. (Courtesy Nassau County Archives.)

Peter Crosby Barnum (1816–1889), who was no relation to circus great P.T. Barnum, was the largest landowner in East Meadow—and in all of Queens County. He and his wife, Sarah Ann, had a model farm on more than 2,000 acres up and down Barnum (Merrick) Avenue that she inherited from her father. P.C. Barnum was a wealthy clothier in New York City's Bowery but eventually gave up that business to oversee the hundreds of employees required to work the farm and take his produce to the Wallabout Market in Brooklyn. He became president of the Queens County Agricultural Society. (Courtesy Nassau County Archives.)

Sarah Ann Barnum (1814–1893) was the daughter of Thomas and Susan Baldwin, for whom Baldwin is named. She became one of the most influential women in the history of Queens County. Not only did she raise children and operate the family's large estate, she was also a civic leader, philanthropist, and visionary. When she learned of bad conditions in almshouses, Barnum cut red tape and bought 450-acre Hog Island (near Long Beach) for use as the Queens County Poor Farm, turning it over to the county for no profit. Today, it is known as Barnum Island. (Courtesy Patrick Barnum.)

The Barnum estate, seen above around 1905, was an impressive homestead on today's Barnum Woods site, west of Merrick Avenue. While P.C. Barnum was employed in New York City, Sarah Ann raised hundreds of purebred horses and cattle, ran a dairy, grew vegetables, and oversaw hundreds of employees. Her home had a library and cupola to look out upon her estate. West of the house, at the Meadow Brook, was a gristmill used by many East Meadow farmers. The Barnums' children remained active in the family estate for many years, first Joshua Willets Barnum and then Kate Vail Barnum, seen as a child in 1865 below with her brother. Kate, an expert horse rider, owned many parcels of land. The main estate itself was leassed to John W. Munson in 1908. Joshua's daughter Maie built a second mansion in 1915 and trained police dogs in her kennels, which later became the Silas Andrews "cattery" called Sunny Knoll. It was finally sold off for residential development around 1952. (All, courtesy Nassau County Archives.)

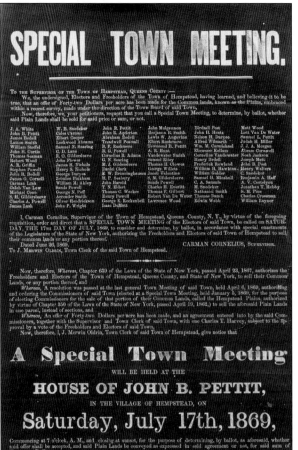

SPECIAL TOWN MEETING.

To the Supervisor of the Town of Hempstead, Queens County:—
We, the undersigned, Electors and Freeholders of the Town of Hempstead, having learned, and believing it to be true, that an offer of Forty-two Dollars per acre has been made for the Common lands, known as the Plains, embraced within a recent survey, made under the direction of the Town Board of said Town,
Now, therefore, we, your petitioners, request that you call a Special Town Meeting, to determine, by ballot, whether said Plain Lands shall be sold for said price or sum, or not.

J. A. White	W. B. Snedeker	John R. Pettit	John Mulgannon	Birdsall Post	Mott Wood
John B. Pettit	Coles Carman	John R. Appleton	Benjamin R. Smith	John H. Hentz	Lott Van De Water
James Bedell	Elbert Cooper	Abraham Bedell	Lewis W. Angevine	Nelson H. Duryee	Samuel L. Pettit
Lotton Smith	Lockwood Abrams	Treadwell Pearsall	Ebert Rushmore	Alfred Wilmarth	Judah H. Miller
William Stoffel	Samuel N. Searing	R. F. Rushmore	Townsend R. Pettit	Wm. M. Carmichael	J. J. A. Morgan
John H. Curtis	C. D. Lane	R. G. Powell	A. R. Hunt	Ebenezer Kellum	Abram Cornwell
Thomas Seaman	R. O. Gildersleeve	Cornelius B. Adams	Vandewater Smith	Cornelius Vandewater	Noah Jackson
Robert Wood	John Flower	G. N. Searing	Samuel Riley	Henry Bedell	Joseph Mott
A. R. Griffin	James H. Nichols	M. J. Gildersleeve	Thomas H. Clowes	Frederick Rowland	John B. Post
Stephen Powell	Henry S. Nichols	Daniel Clark	George Willets	William H. Hawkins	Henry Walters
John R. Bedell	George Duryea	E. W. Braeninghausen	Jacob Valentine	William Golder	C. Snedeker
James G. Cornell	Zebulon Pinkham	H. P. Seabury	S. M. Gildersleeve	Samuel H. Mixshall	Benjamin A. Haff
Carman Losh	William M. Axley	John Harold	Smith Powell	C. A. Samnis	A. V. Cortelyou
Caleb Van Low	Sands Powell	T. N. Elderd	Charles H. Everitt	M. Snedeker	Jonathan T. Hebby
Michael Coon	George N. Pell	Thomas C. Weeker	Thomas F. Gilbert	Nathaniel Smith	S. M. Pine
S. H. Gildersleeve	Arrender Smith	Henry Powell	Robert Van De Water	Thomas Dutch	Charles Crossman
Charles A. Powell	Oliver Hendrickson	George E. Rockenbell	Lawrence Wood	Edwin Webb	William Raynor
James Losh	John P. Wright	Isaac DeMott			

I, Carman Cornelius, Supervisor of the Town of Hempstead, Queens County, N. Y., by virtue of the foregoing requisition, order and direct that a SPECIAL TOWN MEETING of the Electors of said Town, be called on SATURDAY, THE 17th DAY OF JULY, 1869, to consider and determine, by ballot, in accordance with special enactments of the Legislature of the State of New York, authorizing the Freeholders and Electors of said Town of Hempstead to sell their common lands or any portion thereof.
Dated June 26, 1869.   CARMAN CORNELIUS, Supervisor.
To J. Merwin Oldrin, Town Clerk of the said Town of Hempstead.

Now, therefore, Whereas, Chapter 639 of the Laws of the State of New York, passed April 23, 1867, authorizes the Freeholders and Electors of the Town of Hempstead, Queens County, and State of New York, to sell their Common Lands, or any portion thereof, and
Whereas, A resolution was passed at the last general Town Meeting of said Town, held April 6, 1869, authorizing and ordering the Commissioners of said Town (elected at a Special Town Meeting, held January 5, 1869, for the purpose of electing Commissioners for the sale of that portion of their Common Lands, called the Hempstead Plains, authorized by virtue of Chapter 350 of the Laws of the State of New York, passed April 10, 1862,) to sell the aforesaid Plain Lands in one parcel, instead of sections, and
Whereas, An offer of Forty-two Dollars per acre has been made, and an agreement entered into by the said Commissioners, together with the Supervisor and Town Clerk of said Town, with one Charles T. Harvey, subject to the approval by a vote of the Freeholders and Electors of said Town,
Now, therefore, I, J. Merwin Oldrin, Town Clerk of said Town of Hempstead, give notice that

A Special Town Meeting

WILL BE HELD AT THE

HOUSE OF JOHN B. PETTIT,

IN THE VILLAGE OF HEMPSTEAD, ON

Saturday, July 17th, 1869,

Commencing at 7 o'clock, A. M., and closing at sunset, for the purpose of determining, by ballot, as aforesaid, whether said offer shall be accepted, and said Plain Lands be conveyed as expressed in said agreement or not, for said sum of Forty-two Dollars per acre.
Dated June 26th, 1869.
                                                                          J. MERWIN OLDRIN, Town Clerk.

From Colonial times, the farmers of the Hempstead Plains (above) kept common grazing lands in the East Meadow Hollow. Strict regulations existed on the maintenance of fences around the common lands. Each year on the last Monday in October, farmers would collect their marked cattle and sheep from pasture in this public pen, and the event became known as "Parting Day" or "Sheep Parting Day." Eventually, this day would be filled with carnival-like celebrations. In 1869, Sarah Ann Barnum orchestrated one of the most important land deals in town history—the sale of the common lands to benefit public schools and the poor. She convinced the townsfolk to sell the 7,170-acre plains for $55 per acre to Alexander T. Stewart. "The Purchase" (public notice, left) enabled Stewart to build Garden City and paved the way for all future development of the East Meadow area. (Both, courtesy Nassau County Archives.)

Just north of the Barnum estate was Brookholt Mansion, designed by architect Richard Howland Hunt for Oliver Hazard Perry Belmont and Alva Vanderbilt Belmont in 1897. This Colonial Revival mansion, seen above around 1902, was a Gilded Age masterpiece, one of Alva's nine homes. She was a regular New York City socialite with a mansion in Newport, Rhode Island, who orchestrated a loveless marriage between her daughter Consuelo and Charles Spencer-Churchill, an English duke. Her new husband, Oliver, was the son of August Belmont of the Rothschild banking enterprise. August made his fortune financing Japanese expansion after his father-in-law Commodore Matthew Perry had opened up that country to American trade. Together, Alva and Oliver created one of the "show places of America," according to the *New York Times*, on 240 acres of gardens, orchards, and trees, along with stables and other buildings. The pair became very progressive. Oliver began a political campaign against robber barons of the day, and Alva, seen below around 1910, was a suffragette. She served as school trustee and utilized her position of wealth and power to rebuild the Methodist church on Newbridge Avenue. (Above, courtesy Art Kleiner; below, courtesy Library of Congress, Bain Collection.)

Entrance to Brookholt Park, Hempstead, N. Y.

Brookholt's impressive gates are seen above in a c. 1902 postcard. The mansion hosted social gatherings and local fundraisers. In time, the Belmonts' land holdings increased to 800 acres. Willie K. Vanderbilt II, Alva's son, spent considerable amounts of time in East Meadow because of his enthusiasm for early automobiles. He established the Vanderbilt Cup Races in 1904. These races, which took place on public roads, were fast and dangerous but helped the local economy by bringing spectators who spent money on food and lodging. Brookholt's Winter Gardens were located in the impressive structure seen below on the north side of Front Street. In 1915, the estate was sold to Alexander Smith Cochran, who in turn sold to Coldstream Golf Club. The house burned down in 1934 after the discovery of an elaborate Prohibition-era still. (Both, courtesy Art Kleiner.)

The Winter Gardens, Brookholt, Hempstead, N. Y.

In 1908, O.H.P. Belmont died from complications from appendicitis, and his wife, Alva, attempted to sell the estate. After failing to find a buyer, she began a short-lived but much-publicized venture, Mrs. Belmont's Farm for Women. The training farm's mission was to take women out of monotonous city factory work and teach them a self-sustaining trade in the fresh country air. According to Alva, it was "a simple way to earn a good living . . . competent to take places such as men fill now . . . paid just what men get." A young women's training school was not a stretch for Alva, as she was an outspoken suffragette. She marched in suffrage parades in Hempstead and Manhattan and empowered women to vote in local elections where they were already enfranchised. The house itself was used as a meeting place for leaders in the suffrage movement. (Both, courtesy Library of Congress, Bain Collection.)

Arthur Brisbane (1864–1936) was a famous journalist who worked for Joseph Pulitzer and then William Randolph Hearst. After achieving significant success reaching an estimated 30 million readers daily, Brisbane made a fortune in New York City real estate. A great horseman and farmer and believer in Long Island's future, Brisbane called East Meadow his home and commuted to New York City by train. One of his residences was next to the O.H.P. Belmont mansion at the intersection of Front Street and Barnum (Merrick) Avenue, later the site of Waldbaum's. He had an estate near the entrance to today's Eisenhower Park, just next to "East Meadows," the home of his personal attorney Geoffrey Konta (1887–1942). (Courtesy Library of Congress.)

Half Way Nirvana was the country home of Elliott Roosevelt. It was built on 10 acres in the Salisbury section of East Meadow at the northwest corner of Newbridge Avenue (now Salisbury Park Drive) and Valentines Road. Elliott was Teddy Roosevelt's brother who enjoyed fox hunting, polo, and riding—all sporting activities at the Meadowbrook Hunt Club just down the road. His daughter (Anna) Eleanor (1884–1962), who spent her childhood at the estate between 1888 and 1892, grew up to become first lady and an international rights activist. She is pictured at center. Faced with multiple personal losses, including his wife, child, and familial respect, Elliott died from alcoholism and drug abuse. Eleanor and her sister Gracie moved in with their grandmother. (Courtesy National Archives and Records Administration.)

The Oasis, just southeast of Half Way Nirvana in the Salisbury section, was the longtime home of Emily Louise Ladenburg, widow of Moritz Adolph Ladenburg, who was lost at sea in 1896. Adolph, a Jewish-German banker, joined with Ernst Thalmann, an American banker, to form Ladenburg Thalmann in 1876. In time, the company grew into a major international financial services firm. Emily was an expert horseback rider who wore a split skirt and helped end the sidesaddle style of riding to liberate women. The estate featured the Ladenburg Race Track, where people would come to ride in style. Houses were built in the family's Meadow Brook Park Colony next to trees imported from Europe. Above, a home on the property known as The Box is seen around 1930. Below, the Long Island Motor Parkway at Stewart Avenue, just south of the Oasis, is pictured in 1908. The property was sold to F. William Boelson and again for postwar development in 1950. The Salisbury School was built on the oval racetrack. (Above, courtesy Nassau County Archives; below, courtesy Howard Kroplick.)

Joseph John "J.J." Lannin (1866–1928) rose out of poverty to become a business tycoon worth $7 million. Lannin walked from his native Québec to Boston as a teenager and became a baseball player, eventually owning the Boston Red Sox. He most notably brought novice Babe Ruth into the club and developed him into a famous player. Lannin was an avid golfer and developed great golf courses, including the five at Salisbury Golf Club in East Meadow. Pictured below is the estate of Dorothy Lannin, which sits in East Meadow's Eisenhower Park. The home was given to Dorothy as a wedding gift by her late father, J.J. Lannin. The home served as the county museum and later as the headquarters for the Women's Sports Foundation. (Above, courtesy Library of Congress, Bain Collection; below, courtesy Nassau County Archives.)

J.J. Lannin turned his endeavors to the real estate market and became the owner of several hotels. The Salisbury Golf Club was originally built in 1917 as private links for his swanky Garden City Hotel. Living and working near several important airfields, it was only natural that he became involved with airplane travel. Lannin acquired Roosevelt Field and walked Charles Lindbergh to the *Spirit of St. Louis* for his famous 1927 transatlantic flight. Fate would not be kind to the Lannins. J.J. fell or jumped from the ninth floor of his Hotel Granada in Brooklyn. His children took over the golf course, seen above in 1925, but could not afford to pay the back taxes. The property was purchased by Nassau County in 1940, and Salisbury (now Eisenhower) Park was opened in 1944. At right, Dorothy Lannin Tunstall is pictured with her children Harry and Joan outside their East Meadow home around 1935. (Above, courtesy Gary Hammond; right, courtesy Nassau County Archives.)

The beautiful Salisbury Clubhouse, which was located just west of Merrick Avenue, is seen in these postcards from 1925. Before becoming a golf clubhouse, the building was Lannin's Hotel. Of the five golf courses built at Salisbury, number four exists today as Eisenhower Park's 18-hole Red Course. Designed by Devereux Emmet, the course was played by wealthy and connected high-society athletes from its opening in 1914. The Roaring Twenties was the decade of highlight for the golf club, for it was in 1926 that famed PGA golfer Walter Hagen won his $11,100 championship at Salisbury. The Salisbury Clubhouse was sold and used for industry through the 1980s before being demolished. Another clubhouse, known today as the Carltun, existed for public players. (Both, courtesy Gary Hammond.)

A 3962 Meadow Brook Club, Hempstead, L. I.

The Meadow Brook Hunt Club began in 1881 and gradually expanded through the early 20th century. Its clubhouse was near that of Salisbury, west of Merrick Avenue and south of Stewart Avenue. Club members enjoyed cross-country runs chasing hounds over the brushy plains of the former common lands of East Meadow and neighboring communities, often as far as Plainedge (so named because it was the edge of the prairie). Members on horseback would face challenging turf, fences, and galloping horses as they hunted for foxes. Maps dating from 1886 show the Meadow Brook Hunt lands in the A.T. Stewart purchase area over today's Eisenhower Park. The hunts were purely sporting events, but they served a more practical purpose as well: an 1896 *New York Times* article reported on the local farmers complaining of an increase in foxes and the loss of dozens of chickens. (Above, courtesy Art Kleiner; right, courtesy Nassau County Archives.)

By the turn of the 20th century, polo had become a fashionable sport among the Long Island elite. This map of "Polo Land" shows an early 1900s Nassau County with a significant number of polo fields. The Meadow Brook Hunt Club turned into a more comprehensive club and was one of the largest and most significant fields within the county. Served by the Long Island Motor Parkway and the Central Branch of the Long Island Rail Road, city dwellers could easily traverse the Long Island countryside to enjoy watching a match. Sportsmen, socialites, and even important politicians such as Theodore Roosevelt regularly attended. (Courtesy Art Kleiner.)

0804...I-876F-8)(7-30-36-10-30A)(12-1000) MITCHEL F'LD, N.Y.

Not limited to polo, the Meadow Brook Club built its first golf course in 1894. The course stretched from Stewart Avenue to Hempstead Turnpike, west of Merrick Avenue. The Meadow Brook Club and the Cold Stream Golf Course, its neighbor to the south, were taken by eminent domain to begin building the extension of the Meadowbrook Parkway in 1953. That year, the Meadow Brook Club moved to Jericho. In this aerial photograph from 1936, the Meadow Brook Club is seen just north and east of Mitchel Field. The main clubhouse and international polo fields were located south of Stewart Avenue. Additional facilities were located north of Stewart. Garden City can be seen on the top of the map, as can Roosevelt Field. Merrick Avenue can be seen on the bottom, along with the Salisbury Golf Course. (Courtesy Howard Kroplick.)

Above, the Meadow Brook Club House is seen as it appeared between 1910 and 1915. The clubhouse was built from an old farmhouse and expanded to include polo grounds, tennis courts, a golf course, and even a dairy. Below, players compete in the international polo match at Meadow Brook field in June 1913. (Both, courtesy Library of Congress, Bain Collection.)

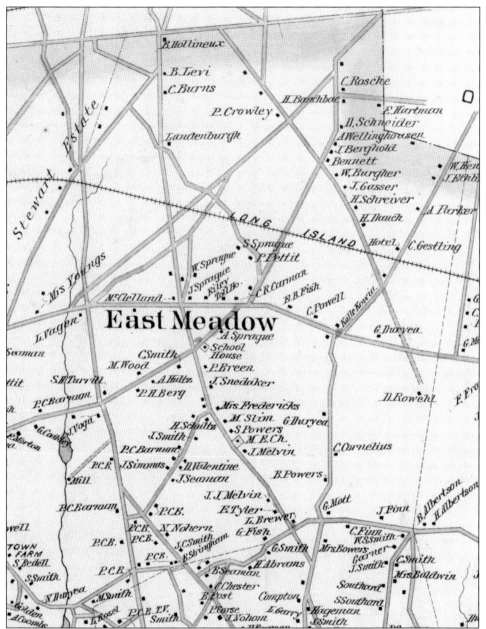

This 1891 map shows East Meadow at a time of great transformation. Families long established would begin to farm and reside next to more recent arrivals. Many German names would emerge on maps of East Meadow, a reflection of larger immigration patterns to the United States. The A.T. Stewart estate can be seen on the northwest corner of the map. Roads that traversed the old common lands (near today's Eisenhower Park) would soon disappear. The Barnum estate was at the height of its influence, with properties on both sides of current-day Merrick and Bellmore Avenues. The small cemetery across from the Barnum mansion was eventually emptied, the remains exhumed and reinterred in Greenfield Cemetery in Uniondale. Interesting landmarks include the Newbridge Hotel, District No. 3 schoolhouse, Methodist Episcopal church, Barnum's mill, and Town Farm, now A. Holly Patterson Extended Care Facility. (Courtesy New York Public Library.)

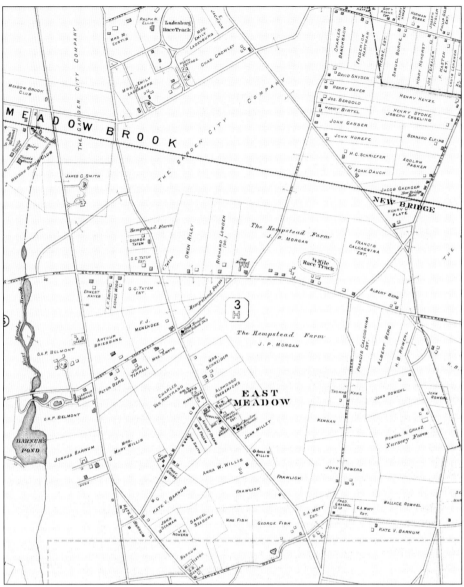

The Gilded Age of East Meadow is seen here in the large estates of O.H.P. Belmont, Arthur Brisbane, James C. Smith, and Emily Ladenburg that had been established by 1906. The Barnum estate was divided between Joshua Barnum and Kate Vail Barnum, both of whom lived in the area long after their parents' property was broken up. J.P. Morgan of banking fame owned many acres of land called Hempstead Farm, which had been a major dog breeding operation under Thomas Terry. A horse racing track was built on his property where Meadowbrook Hospital eventually rose. Relatives of the Morgan family were active in the Meadow Brook Club, seen west of Merrick Avenue. The Hempstead Turnpike, having been turned over to Nassau County, ceased to operate as a corporation and no tollbooth can be seen. It was replaced by a dog kennel. Stewart Avenue now traversed the lands where hunting and shepherding were once common. At the time of this map's printing, James Clinch Smith was engaged in a lengthy legal battle to secure his property from the will of his relatives, Alexander T. and Cornelia Clinch Stewart. His brother-in-law was famed architect Stanford White. (Courtesy Stony Brook University.)

Three

PLANES, TRAINS, AND THE GREAT AUTOMOBILE

A Remington-Burnelli transport plane flies over the Hempstead Plains in 1925. Because of the flat, open land, Long Island was a major center for air travel and military defense in the early days of flight. This view looks east over East Meadow. The Salisbury Club can be seen at center, and the Meadowbrook Club is visible at bottom right. The Central Line of the Long Island Rail Road runs from top to bottom, with the Salisbury Plains station near the intersection of Merrick Avenue. (Courtesy Nassau County Archives.)

Car enthusiast and heir to industrial fortune Willie K. Vanderbilt Jr. enjoyed racing his automobiles, so much that he was cited for dangerous speeds on local roads. This prompted him to construct a private highway, free from law enforcement and other encumbrances. The Long Island Motor Parkway, which opened on October 10, 1908, would serve two purposes: as the host of the Vanderbilt Cup Races and, eventually, as a toll road from Queens to Long Island's golf and polo clubs. The parkway was truly the first modern controlled-access road. The concrete pavement, elimination of grade crossings, and no speed limit allowed motorists to enjoy a high-quality, fast ride for those who could afford its steep toll of $2. The toll dropped to 40¢ through the 1930s as driving became more commonplace and quality highways, such as the Northern State Parkway, were opened to the public. Drivers entered the highway at lodges, such as the Meadow Brook Lodge at Merrick Avenue seen here. (Both, courtesy Howard Kroplick.)

The Vanderbilt Cup Races were exciting and dangerous. Local residents flocked to the 65 bridges to watch the race, and flagmen were hired to warn onlookers of speeding vehicles. Above, a vehicle approaches Merrick Avenue during the 1910 race. The bridge itself caused several accidents on Merrick Avenue because of its narrow opening. Below, a quieter scene transpires on the Long Island Motor Parkway as a Buick crosses over Westbury Road (now Old Westbury Road), just west of Newbridge Road. This bridge was one of the original 16 constructed in 1908; it was still in operation for Salisbury Park Drive in the 1950s. Stretching almost 50 miles from Queens to Suffolk, the Long Island Motor Parkway was used by more than 150,000 cars from 1924 to 1930 before closing in 1938. (Both photographs from the Hayden Allen Collection, courtesy Howard Kroplick.)

Charles Kiestling built the New Bridge Hotel at the intersection of Newbridge Road and the Central Line in 1874. It was later operated by Jacob Gaenger and was a good place to watch the Vanderbilt Cup Races along the Long Island Motor Parkway. Today, this site is directly north of Salisbury Park Drive, the old motor parkway. Above, George Saltzman is shown driving the No. 12 Thomas racer during the 1908 race. Below, Newbridge Road is pictured in a view looking north. The Central Line runs nearly parallel to the Long Island Motor Parkway, with the New Bridge Hotel on the other side of the bridge. (Both, courtesy Howard Kroplick.)

Bridge at Newbridge Rd. Aug. 20 '08

A.T. Stewart planned the Central Rail Road of Long Island in 1871 to take his Garden City residents to New York City. The line, along with the Flushing & North Side Rail Road, was a competitor to the Long Island Rail Road's Hempstead Branch. On August 1, 1873, "Stewart's Railroad" was extended from Hempstead to Babylon, not far from where Stewart had a brickyard used for the construction of Garden City. The railroad ran right through the heart of the Hempstead Plains, which he had purchased in 1869. Stations were built at Meadow Brook (Salisbury Plains) and New Bridge Road. In 1886, the Long Island Rail Road acquired his railroad. A new station at Salisbury Plains was built at Merrick Avenue in 1917 (above) and rebuilt in 1923 (below). After service was discontinued in 1939, the structure became a private residence. (Both, courtesy Art Huenke.)

The Central Railroad's extension east of Garden City was taken out of service in 1939 but used again briefly beginning in 1946, as Levittown required the delivery of massive amounts of construction materials for the new development. Right-of-way exists today in Eisenhower Park and along high-voltage power lines through Levittown and Bethpage. To commemorate the importance of railroad travel and the development of the Hempstead Plains, Long Island Rail Road's Engine No. 35 was donated to Nassau County and displayed in Salisbury (Eisenhower) Park from 1956 to 1979. Engine No. 35, used from 1928 to 1955, was the very last steam locomotive to operate on Long Island. Many children of the 1950s remember the locomotive's move to the park, as seen above. Below, county executive A. Holly Patterson can be seen at the microphone. (Both, courtesy Nassau County Archives.)

A Douglas C-29 Dolphin and Fokker Y1C-14 fly over East Meadow in this aerial view from 1935. The hamlet's proximity to two major airfields—Mitchel Field to the west and Roosevelt Field to the northwest—made East Meadow an excellent place for viewing both military and civilian aircraft. Both airports can be seen at the top of this picture. The road running diagonally up the center, from bottom left to top right, is Newbridge (now East Meadow) Avenue. In the distance is Merrick Avenue. At bottom left, both the Methodist Episcopal and Polish National Churches are visible near Hoeffner's farmlands. Early suburban development is seen to the right, southeast of Prospect Avenue. Coldstream Golf Club is north of Hempstead Turnpike, the central left-right (west-east) road in this picture. The area between Front Street and Hempstead Turnpike was primarily farmland. Hidden behind the No. 99 plane was the East Meadow Public School No. 1, the site of today's East Meadow Public Library. (Courtesy Art Kleiner.)

Most suburbanites think of Garden City's Roosevelt Field as a tremendous shopping mall, but its name comes from the important airfield that existed on the property, and that of the future Roosevelt Raceway, for the first half of the 20th century. The field was owned by rags-to-riches entrepreneur Joseph J. Lannin. Roosevelt Field's most notable takeoff was that of Charles A. Lindbergh on May 20, 1927, as seen in these photographs. "Lucky Lindy" flew alone nonstop to Paris, France, in 33.5 hours, becoming a national hero and worldwide sensation with his plane, the *Spirit of St. Louis*. Lindbergh flew directly over East Meadow as soon as he took off, helping to usher in a period of record-breaking air feats. Roosevelt Field, which operated from 1916 to 1951, was a takeoff point for Amelia Earhart, Wiley Post, and other figures of the Roaring Twenties. (Both, courtesy Library of Congress.)

Long before Mitchel Field served the United States as an air force base (1918–1961), the area made its mark as a military post. There was an enlistment center during the Revolutionary War; later came Camp Winfield Scott and Camp Black. Eventually, the area was part of a larger military aerodrome installation that included Camp Mills and Roosevelt Field, then known as Hazelhurst Field. Mitchel Field was the second such field, renamed for former New York City mayor John P. Mitchel. As Mitchel Field expanded greatly in the interwar period, new barracks, hangars, warehouses, offices, and even officers' club facilities were built, partially encompassing the old Meadow Brook Club. In 1941, the government acquired the Cold Stream Golf Course for expansion. These images show training activities in 1942. (Both, courtesy Library of Congress.)

Barracks and military housing for Mitchel Field existed at several facilities in East Meadow, including the Santini Sub Base (below) and Mitchel Manor. The New Cantonment Hospital at Santini served the needs of wounded soldiers returning from the battlefields of World War II. The East Meadow facilities were severed from the main base when the Meadowbrook Parkway extension opened in 1956. A "bridge to nowhere" connects the two sides today. A spectacular fire in 1977 claimed the old wooden barracks on the northwest corner of Merrick Avenue and Front Street. Part of the Mitchel Manor complex still serves as housing for military personnel. The majority of Mitchel Field is now part of Hofstra University, Nassau County Community College, Nassau Coliseum, and the Cradle of Aviation Museum. The photograph above shows Mitchel Field in 1939, before major expansion across the Meadow Brook, seen running through the Cold Stream and Meadow Brook Clubs. (Both, courtesy Howard Kroplick.)

Training and experimental flights were common at Mitchel Field. One of the most notable events at the airport was the crash of Ben Kelsey's Lockheed XP-38 on February 11, 1939. Built under tight secrecy, the two-engine fighter was the fastest and most up-to-date secret weapon of the Air Force. After a record-breaking 7.5-hour transcontinental flight from March Field in California, Kelsey crashed onto the Cold Stream Golf Course as he attempted to land. He survived and the Lightning program was a success. (Courtesy US Army.)

Throughout the 1940s and 1950s, plane crashes plagued East Meadow, a fact that led to the closure of Mitchel Field in 1961. In 1943, two planes collided, one crashing at Merrick Avenue and Front Street, the other at Hempstead Turnpike and East Meadow Avenue. A 1948 incident occurred at Merrick Avenue and Front Street. In 1955, this B-26 bomber crashed into a house on Barbara Drive, killing only the pilots. A similar accident took place on Prospect Avenue in 1962. Many witnesses walking to the East Meadow Jewish Center remember the horrible crash that claimed the life of 14-month-old Eric Shapiro. (Courtesy East Meadow Fire District.)

As the early era of flight came to a close on Long Island and suburban development took hold, the construction of controlled-access highways began in earnest. Constructed in the 1930s, the parkways were originally designed by master builder Robert Moses, pictured in 1939, to take city dwellers to his Long Island parks. Moses designed most of the infrastructure of New York City and Long Island for decades. His local projects, such as the Southern State, Northern State (which originally included the Wantagh as an extension), and Meadowbrook Parkways (extended between the Northern and Southern Parkways in 1953) enabled suburbanites to travel great distances in considerably less time. The parkways also helped to define the borders of unincorporated East Meadow. (Courtesy Library of Congress.)

Seen here is the construction of the East Meadow exit of the Southern State Parkway at Newbridge Road in 1929. Note the WEAF radio towers in the distance. (Courtesy Nassau County Archives.)

Four

KEEPING EAST MEADOW SAFE

Volunteers of the East Meadow Fire Department line up at a parade in front of headquarters on Newbridge (East Meadow) Avenue in the 1950s. This building was erected in 1948. The fire department has been a point of pride for the district since residents first organized volunteer companies in 1921. Advancements in training and technology enabled the department to modernize throughout the decades. The first alarms were sounded by hitting two iron hoops on Prospect Avenue and Roslyn Place with sledgehammers. Before the completion of the Water District in 1951, the few available hydrants were fed from local wells. (Courtesy East Meadow Fire District.)

Before incorporating as an official fire district, civic leaders in East Meadow saw the need for fire protection in the growing community. In 1921, a Firemen's Association was organized; a small building on Maple Avenue was erected the following year. Two companies of volunteers served the hamlet over the next eight years. Frederick Bickmeyer donated the first truck, which was kept in his garage. The East Meadow Fire District, as seen below, was officially formed on February 2, 1930. Three weeks later, a meeting was held at the Maple Avenue Fire Hall to elect commissioners of the new fire district, and 162 residents cast their ballots. The first five commissioners were familiar East Meadow names: Frederick Bickmeyer, Martin Marcinkowski, William Maitland, William Lowden, and Louis Schneider. Above, firefighters train on their 1917 Mack ladder truck near Station 2 in 1937; the truck had been purchased from Franklin Square in 1929. (Above, courtesy Nassau County Archives; below, courtesy East Meadow Fire District.)

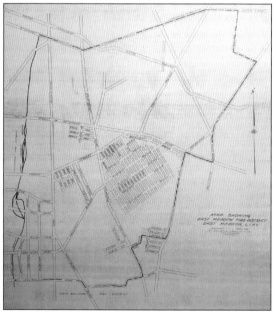

The original Firemen's Association housed its apparatus in volunteers' homes and garages, but the new department needed a permanent firehouse. District voters approved a fire station at Newbridge (East Meadow) and Park Avenues, along with the purchase of a pumper truck. A modern alarm was later installed on top of the white building, seen above in 1939. This modest station served the community until after World War II. At that time, exponential growth in housing necessitated more substantial fire coverage. Although commissioners acquired the property for a headquarters building in 1936, they had to wait until 1947 for voters to approve a new firehouse. The Front Street School can be seen next to the alarm tower in the 1948 photograph below. Two additional garages were built on the left side of the headquarters building in the 1960s. (Above, courtesy Hoeffner Family; below, courtesy East Meadow Fire District.)

Rapid development in the Levittown areas of East Meadow led to the addition of two company houses in the northeastern section of the district. Station No. 3 was built on land donated by Levitt, next to the old Long Island Rail Road Central Line on Newbridge Road. A Quonset hut, seen above around 1950, served the department until voters approved a permanent building, constructed in 1959. A large bond issue passed in 1951 added Station No. 4 on Carman Avenue and Gasser Avenue (Old Westbury Road/Bob Reed Lane). Further expansion of these firehouses followed in the early 1970s. Below is the new Station No. 2 house "wetdown" in 1972. Areas in the northern section of Salisbury are served by the Westbury and Hicksville districts. (Both, courtesy East Meadow Fire District.)

The 1951 bond issue helped purchase three new pumpers and much-needed communications systems. Above, a 1950s engine pumper heads to the scene of a fire. Below, Chief Dominick Santoro poses in front of his car in 1956. The commissioners have adopted a policy of replacing outdated fire trucks every 20 years, assuring up-to-date equipment for East Meadow's protection. (Both, courtesy East Meadow Fire District.)

A telephone alarm system was installed in East Meadow in 1957. Along with this improvement, call boxes were installed on the street. With these telephones, residents could contact the fire department, Meadowbrook Hospital, or the water department. Officials partnered with the public schools to instruct children in the use of the new system. Below, the fire chief enjoys the attention of the local ladies while sitting in his truck in front of the Hoeffner homestead. (Both, courtesy East Meadow Fire District.)

Here, the tournament team known as the Meadowlarks celebrates its 1958 victory. Originally known as the Suicide Squad, the training team won local firefighting contests year after year, including a statewide win in 1946. Arthur Brisbane donated a Pierce Arrow, the first competition truck. Not to be outdone, the Ladies' Auxiliary won many awards for appearances in fire parades. The important work of the auxiliary has assisted the department since 1924. From left to right below, firefighters E. Ackerly Sr., B. Cannon, J. Kusen, and F. Esposito lead the way as the firemen's band follows. The ladies would not be far behind. (Both, courtesy East Meadow Fire District.)

E.ACKERLY Sr, B.GANNON, J.KUSEN, F.ESPOSITO

Rows of ranch houses line Prospect Avenue where a firemen's parade marches by in the 1950s. J. Delaney leads the way with the first Duke. At the time, the fire department kept a dalmatian on hand; several dogs named Duke served East Meadow. Parades are still an important feature of East Meadow civic pride, with yearly celebrations of Veterans Day and homecoming. (Courtesy East Meadow Fire District.)

In this view looking north up Carman Avenue in 1957, the newly constructed $4.5 million Nassau County Correctional Center can be seen just north of a recently expanded Meadowbrook Hospital. Before the jail was built, the county sent inmates from Mineola to work the land on the Nassau County Prison Farm. Under the supervision of experienced farmers, the prisoners grew vegetables that supplied the jail, Meadowbrook Hospital, a children's shelter, and local tuberculosis sanatorium. Also seen is East Meadow High School, only two years old at the time. (Courtesy Nassau County Archives.)

Meadowbrook Hospital opened as a 200-bed county hospital in 1935 after four years of planning and construction. The land and buildings cost almost $1.9 million, an enormous sum for Depression-era rural America. In its first year, Meadowbrook Hospital treated fewer than 150 patients a day but had a top-notch staff of 330. Above, residents and interns pose around 1940. Below, the main building facing Hempstead Turnpike at right was architecturally significant, as it was constructed with a solarium on each side. A major expansion in 1950 was responsible for building much of this complex, which was expanded again in 1960. Carman Avenue runs along the bottom. (Above, courtesy Nassau County Archives; below, courtesy Gary Hammond.)

Meadowbrook Hospital became Nassau County Medical Center in 1970 and embarked upon a tremendous building project (above). Its 19-story, $49 million Dynamic Care Building opened in February 1974. Aside from being the tallest building in Nassau County, the hospital became a major teaching facility with 1,200 beds. A Level I trauma center and burn unit rounded out the medical center's primary purpose of providing for the health care needs of county residents, and new hospital affiliations affected a name change to Nassau University Medical Center. While still under construction in July 1970, the Dynamic Care tower suffered a setback—one of the most financially destructive fires in county history. A fire in the tar roof of a four-story section of the new building scorched the steel-and-brick construction (below), melted aluminum panels, and broke windows, prompting an evacuation of the existing hospital building. (Both, courtesy East Meadow Fire District.)

Five

LEARNING AND GROWING IN DISTRICT NO. 3

The East Meadow School District is among the oldest in New York State and has been continuously educating students for more than 200 years. Public schools in the town were first conceived in January 1812 with the passage of New York State's Common School Act. Originally known as Brushy Plains, Common School District No. 3 was one of 13 original districts in the town of Hempstead. Many of these districts remain today, with borders that are remarkably similar to when they were set up in 1814. Until the 20th century, East Meadow's enrollment ranged from about 20 to 110. The district's earliest students were taught in a rural one-room schoolhouse at the corner of Front Street and Newbridge (East Meadow) Avenue. When replaced with a new one-room school, the first building was likely moved to the northwest corner, later the Edward Ryder Farm. (Courtesy Hoeffner family.)

School funding was a mixture of state aid, local tax revenue, and "rate bills" (tuition). Rate bills were eliminated in 1849, enabling the poorest children to attend without paying tuition. In 1867, district voters resolved "that we have a new School House" and the 1868 one-room school was built diagonally across the street for $1,318.76. The school district still owns the property, used today as the East Meadow Public Library. The old building was auctioned off for $57.63. The taxpayers spent their money prudently, and the school was crowded by today's standards, but they did approve of "an instrument of music." (Courtesy Nassau County Archives.)

School attendance for children between 8 and 14 years old became compulsory in 1874. The school population almost doubled that year after town leaders declared that "habitual truants . . . be committed to the Town Poor House," according to the Town of Hempstead records. More books were purchased, but trustees continually voted down new schoolhouse proposals. Finally, a $3,000 bond issue narrowly passed, and this two-room building was constructed in the 1895–1896 school year. The new school, built by E.P. Smith, featured a new fence, a $55 organ, and a $25 bell. The 1868 school was sold for $41 and moved to Newbridge Avenue, as it is seen in the c. 1910 photograph at the top of this page. (Courtesy Gary Hammond.)

The 1895 school (above) had more than 100 children in only two classrooms. In 1900, Mr. W.F. Hill was the principal and Marie Powers (right) was the teacher. At that time, the principal received a $600 yearly salary but was required to perform the duties of custodian and librarian as well as teacher. Miss Powers, who earned $400, taught from approximately 1888 through 1933 and was fondly remembered for her long service. Her car was "fiery red" and was the first in East Meadow. During the 1907–1908 school year, a new $500 steam furnace was installed in the cellar. Children enjoyed playing in the cellar and likely broke the furnace. The trustees demanded that the principal pay half the repair bill, but instead they found themselves looking to hire a new principal at the next board of education meeting. (Both, courtesy Nassau County Archives.)

This beautiful brick edifice was finished in 1911 at a cost exceeding $17,000. The new East Meadow Public School (Front Street School) had four rooms, one of which was used for assembly. The lumber from the 1895 schoolhouse was purchased back by its original builder for $300. An active building campaign by local developers increased the local school population, and the four rooms had become inadequate by 1922. The old 1868 schoolhouse, by then East Meadow Hall, was used temporarily for overflow pupils. Below, first and second grade students are pictured on the Front Street School steps in 1922. (Above, courtesy Nassau County Archives; below, courtesy Hoeffner family.)

In 1922, an additional four classrooms and basement were added to the Front Street School, seen here in 1939. That same year, electric power came to the Front Street area, and kerosene lamps were finally retired. These major upgrades cost $57,000, but additional growth required the district to purchase land on Newbridge Road, an area of significant development. Public School No. 2, Newbridge Road School, opened in 1928, and children occupied the building while a second floor was under construction. For the next 20 years, the population stabilized, and the district educated 400 to 500 students each year. The Newbridge Road School would expand in 1952 and again in 1954. Before the addition of a gymnasium and cafeteria, students used the basement to dance and play. Students brought lunch every day, which was eaten at their desks, and milk could be purchased for a nickel per week. (Both, courtesy East Meadow UFSD No. 3.)

Through the Depression and war years, each building educated students from grades one through eight, with one teacher per grade in each school. Students had many more opportunities than in the past, with an array of clubs at school. By 1933, an instrumental music class and an orchestra had been organized. The 1939–1940 school year saw the beginning of organized physical education classes in East Meadow schools. The teacher Charles Noble taught games and gymnastics and held corrective sessions for children with posture and vision issues. Boys learned boxing and wrestling; girls learned dance. A 1939 student newspaper discusses the fourth grade girls' enthusiasm for learning dances to "Pop Goes the Weasel" and "Jump Jim Crow." Clearly, political correctness was not of paramount importance. These photographs show teachers at the Front Street School in the 1940s (above) and 1950 (below). (Both, courtesy East Meadow UFSD No. 3.)

Students west of Newbridge (East Meadow) Avenue went to the "old school" on Front Street, and students east of the avenue went to the "new school" on Newbridge Road. Coach Noble organized intramural games between the two schools. Eighth grade graduation ceremonies took place in the auditorium of the Newbridge Road School. On December 5, 1950, the Front Street School burned down in a devastating fire, and its 635 students were displaced. The fire could not have happened at a more inopportune time. The district was just beginning a period of runaway population growth, having doubled in two years. The modern buildings were still being planned, and only Prospect Avenue School had recently opened. In an unprecedented move, students went to school on triple session, attending three hours per day, while school officials rushed to plan emergency building programs. The district used space in the Republican Club, Calvary Lutheran Church, and firehouse for makeshift classroom space. Below, Harry Aiosa jokes around in a burned-out classroom. The fire extinguisher still worked! (Above, courtesy Sharon Houghey O'Gara; below, East Meadow UFSD No. 3.)

An endearing custom at the Front Street School was to pick daisies every June and create large daisy chains to decorate the graduation ceremony. After graduating from eighth grade, East Meadow students attended Hempstead High School, the nearest secondary school. The East Meadow Common School District paid tuition to the Hempstead Union Free School District under this arrangement until 1955. The building pictured above housed all grades; it was constructed in 1889 and burned in 1919. On April 10, 1920, ground was broken for the new Hempstead High School seen below. The modern structure opened in 1922 and served as a high school until 1970. According to Joan Oberle, students boarded a "dilapidated old bus" to attend high school. (Both, courtesy Hempstead Public Library.)

Even before the Front Street fire (1950), schools were so overcrowded that classes operated on double session beginning in 1948. The first modern school building in baby-boom East Meadow was the Prospect Avenue School, located north of Coakley Street. The school was not built without controversy. An initial large $900,000 school plan was voted down in early 1948. A smaller 12-classroom building was approved that December. The school was occupied in 1950 but expanded almost immediately in 1951 and then again just three years later. Before East Meadow hired Dr. Edward J. McCleary as the district superintendent in 1951, Frank E. Church was the supervising principal of all schools. Church, who is pictured below with Eleanor Hatzelman-Rhodes in 1952, retired as principal of Prospect Avenue School. (Above, courtesy East Meadow UFSD No. 3; below, courtesy Hatzelman family.)

Creative use of space in the new Prospect Avenue School resulted in 81 students learning in the gymnasium. Above, Margaret Mosher is pictured with her sixth graders in December 1950. Christmas decorations were salvaged from the Front Street School. When Prospect was planned, the district also acquired three other sites: the first was an additional five acres for expansion of the Newbridge Road School, the second was a site on Stewart Avenue for the future Bowling Green Elementary School, and the third was a site near Front Street for a future secondary school known as Meadow Lawn. Below is the last day of school in June 1951. Prospect Avenue and Newbridge Road Schools would fall victim to declining enrollment in the late 1970s. Prospect almost closed in 1975, but the new board reversed the decision. Both were finally shuttered in June 1976. Homes were built on the Prospect property in 1980; the Newbridge building remains as condominiums. (Both, courtesy East Meadow UFSD No. 3.)

Meadow Lawn School, seen above, was occupied in September 1951. It, too, was the subject of taxpayer hesitation. When originally designed, Meadow Lawn was intended to handle students in the elementary and junior high school grades. Before the planning of East Meadow High School began, Meadow Lawn was considered for conversion to a high school once the two new junior high schools were constructed. The original two-story $950,000 secondary school plan was defeated, but a smaller $650,000 building was approved in 1949. The Committee of East Meadow Citizens, working closely with parent groups and the board of education, convinced taxpayers to approve an addition to Meadow Lawn, doubling the size of the school before construction was even completed. Note the red-and-white-striped water tower of the East Meadow Water District, which went into service in 1950 to alleviate persistent droughts. The photograph below is from Margaret Mosher's sixth grade Halloween party in the school's first year. (Both, courtesy East Meadow UFSD No. 3.)

Meadow Lawn School educated students in kindergarten through ninth grade before becoming an elementary school. It was later renamed George H. McVey Elementary School in honor of the influential school board president who oversaw the district's great expansion program. This expansion was more than just buildings. The 1950s brought guidance counselors, school psychologists, vocational education, special education, home tutoring, expanded instruction in art and music, and expanded facilities for physical education. The 1952–1953 school year saw the beginning of adult education, with dozens of teachers instructing hundreds of residents. Teachers, seen above at Meadow Lawn in 1953, were paid between $3,500 and $4,300 per year with opportunities for professional development. Below is a 1954 graduating class. With the opening of government housing at Santini Sub Base and Mitchel Manor, East Meadow's classes began to diversify. (Both, courtesy East Meadow UFSD No. 3.)

Bowling Green School, seen above, first opened on the Stewart Avenue site in the Westbury Estates neighborhood in 1952. It was named after the historical designation for that part of the district. Soaring student enrollment necessitated the construction of a mirror-image building called Bowling Green No. 2 in 1953. A breezeway connected the two identical buildings before an interior hallway was constructed. The K-6 campus cost $2,895,000 and accommodated 1,800 students. In the 1955 aerial photograph below, Bowling Green is at the bottom left (northwest) corner. East Meadow High School and Meadowbrook Elementary School, both just opened, are clearly visible, and Meadowbrook (later McCleary) Junior High School is under construction. Unaltered homes neatly line the new streets. (Above, courtesy East Meadow UFSD No. 3; below, courtesy Nassau County Archives.)

Barnum Woods School was completed in 1954. It is named after the Barnum family that once operated a large farm on the property. Barnum Woods was built by a unique partnership with the state and federal governments. The construction of the tax-exempt Mitchel Manor military housing caused an influx of students. The US government agreed to give the district a $1,025,222.50 grant toward building the $1,327,222 school. Barnum Woods, with its 32 classrooms, gymnasium, health suite, cafetorium, and library, was erected on a 15-acre wooded site. It was the first school in five years to have single-session classes. The building soon proved inadequate. Children in grades four through six were temporarily housed at Woodland, which opened in 1955. Two additions were ultimately built onto the school. Above is a 1954 rendering by Frederic P. Wiedersum, the district's architect. Below, students purchase lunch for 20¢ in 1955. (Both, courtesy East Meadow UFSD No. 3.)

Explosive population growth after World War II led to projections of overcrowding at Hempstead High School, and East Meadow was informed that its students would soon be prohibited from attending. This caused the East Meadow Common School District to change its structure to a Union Free School District on April 28, 1948, expanding the size of the school board from three to five members and paving the way for the planning and construction of the district's first high school. In September 1951, the district purchased a site on Carman Avenue for East Meadow High School, which opened January 31, 1955, at a cost of $3,151,000. "Coeducation is a wonderful thing!" enthused Alexander Crosby in *1955: The Year We Opened Six Schools*. The new high school offered a comprehensive program for both boys and girls, although 20 percent of the boys took vocational training classes in addition to the academic curriculum. (Both, courtesy East Meadow UFSD No. 3.)

The year 1955 was the climax of school construction in East Meadow, with a total of six buildings opening. A record-setting three elementary schools opened on a single day in April: Salisbury, Parkway, and Meadowbrook. Each of these 20-room schools cost $845,298. They were occupied by 1,450 children while the details of the buildings were still being completed. Meadowbrook and Woodland Junior High Schools were opened in September 1955. At that time, elementary schools became K–6 buildings. Neither Salisbury nor Meadowbrook (above) survived a great slump in enrollment in the mid-1970s and early 1980s. Meadowbrook, renamed Edward J. McCleary for the former superintendent, closed in 1982, and a housing development was built on the property. Within 15 years of McCleary's closing, Woodland Junior High (below) was so crowded that a wing had to be constructed in its parking lot. (Above, courtesy Howard Family; below, author's collection.)

Salisbury's closure in 1973 was especially controversial. The board of education was controlled by a conservative organization called Independent Taxpayers of East Meadow, with the aim of reducing property taxes by closing schools. The choice of Salisbury (under construction in 1955) ignited deep-seated socioeconomic tensions in the community. The Salisbury neighborhood of split-level homes was mostly Jewish, liberal, and professional. The older, smaller homes in the Levitt development were largely populated by more conservative, working-class citizens. Their children went to the much larger Bowling Green School and they thought it would be good for the Salisbury children to experience "how the other half lives." Cries of anti-Semitism were heard, and the superintendent Martin T. Walsh courted opinions from civic and religious organizations. The building was rented to the Board of Cooperative Education Services (BOCES) and later became the Leon J. Campo Salisbury Center, the district's administrative offices. Below, students are pictured in a junior high school home economics class. (Both, courtesy East Meadow UFSD No. 3.)

The East Meadow music program is consistently ranked among the finest in the nation. This program has a long history of success and prestige dating back to the creation of a high school in 1955. The program was cultivated by longtime teacher Bill Katz, who came to East Meadow in 1954 and stayed for 40 years. Above, the first high school band students in the district practice on the new field. At the time, only grades nine and ten attended the school; students already enrolled at Hempstead High School completed their education in that district. The following fall, ninth graders attended two new junior high schools. Below, the marching band poses in the music room behind the stage. (Both, courtesy Bill Katz.)

The first complete high school band, with grades 10 through 12, poses outside in 1957. This band was a combination of the two high schools, W. Tresper Clarke having just opened. Among the students seen in this photograph are Ken Sepe, William Tresper Clarke Jr., and Eddie Hoeffner, led by music teacher Bill Katz and director of music John Brierly. Below, the first orchestra is pictured on the stage of East Meadow High School in 1957. Significant funding for the arts would bring large student theatrical performances to East Meadow's theaters, especially under the long tenures of Jared Hershkowitz and Joel Levy. (Both, courtesy Bill Katz.)

W. Tresper Clarke Junior-Senior High School, home of the Rams, opened in the northern section of the district in September 1957. Under the leadership of original principals Samuel Manarel and George Hopke, W.T. Clarke was the first school in the county to offer a full course of study in the technical trades in addition to an academic program. When it opened, student enrollment was 2,440. Within a few years, 2,800 scholars attended Clarke, and the school housed the largest auditorium and gymnasium complex on Long Island. Highlights of Clarke's earlier days were its General Organization (seen below in 1959), Model Congress, Key Club, Dads Club, and Junior High Musical. Clarke was at the center of a notable 1966 legal dispute involving a concert by folk singer Pete Seeger, organized by a community group. The board of education, worried about its political image, canceled the performance. A lawsuit made its way to the state court of appeals, which argued that the district could not discriminate based on the singer's viewpoints. Seeger performed a year later. (Both, courtesy East Meadow UFSD No. 3.)

At right, a student takes a break from class to play guitar outside the extension wings of East Meadow High School around 1973. The East Meadow High School marching bands would go on to win large numbers of Columbus Day parade medals, the choral and orchestral groups would create lasting traditions on both sides of town, and the East Meadow High School band represented the country in an all-expenses-paid trip to Venezuela. In 1968, the city of Barquisimeto invited 65 band students to perform for more than 5,000 people at its annual Festival of the Divine Shepherd. Students explored the country and were treated to parties as if they were celebrities. The Jet Marching Band was the first halftime show at Shea Stadium and would appear again in the 1970s, as seen below. (Right, courtesy Sharon Houghey O'Gara; below, courtesy Bill Katz.)

Peak school enrollment in East Meadow occurred in 1963, when over 19,000 students learned in the district's classrooms. Feeling the effects of the baby boom, East Meadow was the largest school district on Long Island and the third largest in the state. Class sizes were large, as seen here in Mr. Wilson's sixth grade class at Prospect Avenue. Student enrollment at East Meadow High School reached 2,860 for grades 10–12 in 1968. (Courtesy Bernice Carus Lite.)

One staple of high school life in East Meadow is the Battle of the Classes. This spirited sporting competition has connected students to their classmates and school community for many years. This photograph was taken in the East Meadow High School gymnasium in 1976. (Courtesy Mary Ann Messiano Reising.)

The East Meadow Public Library has been an important cultural and geographic center of the community since it opened in April 1955. It came about as a result of a Friends of the Library citizens group. Thomas Dutelle served as the first library director until 1974; early staff members included Frederic Krahn, Laura Seacord, Eileen Holub, Irving Tinyanoff, and Irving Adelman. The library first rented a storefront on Hempstead Turnpike near Meadowbrook Hospital. Another six storefronts were added until the library had grown to a considerable size. Children fondly remember the bookmobile that brought the library to their streets. After several failed attempts, voters approved building a permanent library on the site of the former Front Street School. The library's new home opened in September 1960. A small extension in 1964, a large wraparound expansion in 1986, and total renovation in 2021 created the present building. (Above, courtesy Howard Kroplick; below, courtesy East Meadow Public Library.)

Students are shown here on Wenwood Drive waiting for the kindergarten bus in September 1985. Kindergarten started in East Meadow in the 1947–1948 school year. Previously, the Common School District educated students from grades one through eight. After the 1950 Front Street School fire, classroom space was severely limited, and kindergarten classes were suspended until the 1952–1953 school year. Three years later, the district educated approximately 1,900 kindergarten students. Kindergarten was two half-day sessions, one in the morning and one in the afternoon. Full-day kindergarten began in the 2015–2016 school year with help from the author (right), a member of the school board. (Both, courtesy Eckers Family.)

Six

A SUBURBAN PARADISE

The history of East Meadow as a suburban bedroom community began after World War II. Prior to 1950, small houses dotted streets that were shared with farms. Some of the early suburban streets were laid out after World War I, but these were sparsely populated. Here, Frances Weiner (right) and her friend walk down Elgin Avenue in 1944. (Courtesy Weiner family.)

The first real housing boom in East Meadow occurred after World War I. The United States saw its first suburbs in the Roaring Twenties, and land speculators began purchasing small tracts to lay out dirt streets for development. In order to attract buyers, developers such as the O.L. Schwencke Land and Investment Company planned outings to East Meadow by train from New York City. The first of these developments was called Hempstead Lawns, located west of Newbridge (East Meadow) Avenue to Chestnut Avenue between Prospect Avenue and Front Street. Several more sections of Hempstead Lawns were developed on both sides of Newbridge Avenue in the areas of Stuyvesant and Lenox Avenues. Above is Elmore Avenue in 1940; below is 233 Chestnut Avenue. These rural streets backed up to farmland for many years. (Above, courtesy Weiner family; below, courtesy Jerry Izzo.)

By 1927, planned developments had created a patchwork of small streets along main roads. Hempstead Gardens planned the large project of numbered streets off Prospect Avenue, while Meadowbrook Farms planned a more rural development near Luddington and Richmond Roads. Emphasizing the parklike setting away from the city, developers chose names that evoked a bucolic image: Bellmore Park sprung up along Bellmore Road, and Aviation Park was located off Carman Avenue. Above, Ralph and Carol Lindley are pictured in the backyard of 122 Cambridge Street in a view looking east toward Oxford around 1948; at right, this family portrait was taken at 382 Abington Place of Hempstead Lawns Section No. 9. (Above, courtesy Lindley family; right, courtesy Sharon Houghey O'Gara.)

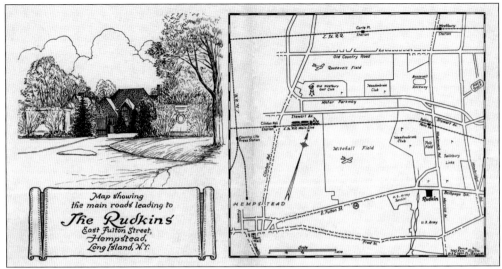

Map showing the main roads leading to *The Rudkins* East Fulton Street, Hempstead, Long Island, N.Y.

An amazing transformation occurred in East Meadow after World War II. The postwar baby boom (1946–1964), coupled with the attractive housing incentives of the GI Bill and overcrowding in places like Brooklyn, brought scores of young families to seek out greener pastures. While 1930s and 1940s East Meadow was made up largely of golf courses, military housing, farms, small developments, and a few fancier homes like the one above (later the Nursing Sisters of the Sick Poor convent), the 1950s brought suburban sprawl. Rows of nearly identical houses were erected in numerous projects. The aerial plan of Salisbury Park Manor, seen below, stressed the proximity to parks, schools, clubhouses, hospitals, horseback riding, and local shopping, all while showing easy access to New York City by car or train. Within 10 years after the war, East Meadow's population increased from about 2,000 to more than 46,000. (Above, courtesy Art Kleiner; below, courtesy Nassau County Archives.)

This 1927 map shows the East Meadow area with post–World War I developments. The various Hempstead Lawn sections were being built off Newbridge Avenue and Newbridge Road, and the East Hempstead Gardens streets were planned north and south of the Prospect Avenue extension. Like later projects mapped out at Bellmore and Prospect Avenues, many of the plans did not come to fruition. Large swaths of this grid would be changed or interrupted by the construction of Meadow Lawn School, the water tower, and neighboring developments. Relatively few houses were built on these streets before the baby boom; those that were constructed often had gardens and livestock in the backyards. (Courtesy New York Public Library.)

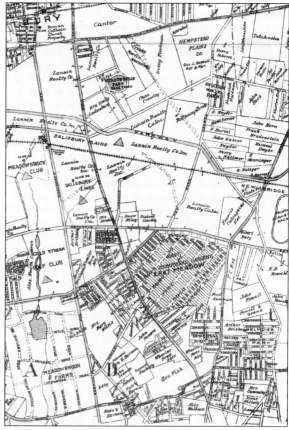

This aerial view from 1955 shows the result of rapid suburban development of the early 1950s. Almost all the houses seen here were part of the Levittown development, which extended into East Meadow (center). The curved streets were designed to reduce speeding and foster a sense of community. A careful examination of this photograph shows the Meadowbrook Elementary School, which had just been completed, and the construction of Meadowbrook (later McCleary) Junior High School. The Clearmeadow development is at bottom left. (Courtesy Nassau County Archives.)

Levittown, begun in 1947, was the first and best-known major planned suburban development in America. A total of 6,000 homes were planned on about 1,000 acres of former potato fields in Island Trees, just east of East Meadow. William Levitt and his family were directly involved in the planning of the community. His brother Alfred designed a 27-step, mass-production construction technique that enabled the company to build 180 homes a week. His father directed the careful landscaping of the lawns—two trees per house. Levitt & Sons bought up forests for lumber, orchestrated exact delivery by train and truck, cut out middlemen by manufacturing their own materials, and changed zoning laws. In doing so, William Levitt made Cape Cod and ranch-style houses affordable to returning veterans. Just $7,990 would buy the original homes, and thousands of people looking for "somewhere that's green" lined up to purchase them on the first day of availability in March 1949. The development, seen here in 1948, grew to 17,000 homes. Restrictive covenants in the deeds prevented the sale of Levittown homes to African Americans, which Levitt saw as a necessity of doing business in a segregated nation. (Courtesy Levittown Public Library.)

Neat rows of new homes were constructed in East Meadow in the early 1950s, some on streets that were originally laid out after World War I. Above, Everett and Laurie Saxton enjoy their new residence on Noble Street near Lenox Estates. Yardwork was especially important to many suburban husbands of the 1950s and 1960s. Since most of the houses looked alike, gardening was one of the only ways to personalize one's home. Phone numbers were through Hempstead, Hicksville, and Wantagh exchanges and could not be dialed directly. In 1948, numbers were standardized to the national format. As the population grew, so did the central offices. These exchange names fostered a sense of community, and East Meadowites were upset in 1952 when they were to be included in the new LEvittown exchange, which they felt devalued their non-Levitt homes. IVanhoe took over for HEmpstead in 1953, and PYramid and EDgewood were introduced in 1954. East Meadow residents could dial nationwide in 1959. (Both, courtesy Tom Saxton.)

We have moved to . . .

DORIS AND EVERETT
SAXTON
1650 NOBLE ST.
EAST MEADOW, N.Y.

Phone IVanhoe 9-3186

Morris Weniger & Sons constructed the Wenwood Oaks "colony" on former farmland off North Jerusalem Road in 1952 and 1953. The 125-house development featured two split-level homes, the Wenwood and the Barden, and one brick ranch called the Glencote. Prices were significantly higher than the neighboring Levitt homes, ranging from $15,950 to $18,250. Like so many split-level homes in the 1950s, Wenwood Oaks featured glazed ceramic tiles, pine-walled dens, and even a laundry chute. Directly adjacent was Jacob Weisbarth's Midland Gardens, with two ranch choices. Veterans were able to purchase these $11,750 and $12,990 homes with only five percent down. (Author's collection.)

David Weisbarth and Irving Newman's large Central Homes development emerged just next to Wenwood Oaks, on the old Fish property. Ranging from $10,690 to $11,790, the 500 ranch-style homes called the Arkansas and the Beaumont included "automatic kitchen equipment" and washing machines. Central Homes would later build split-level homes as well. Nearby, Randal Homes offered 190 "bungalows" in the price range of $8,390 to $8,890. (Author's collection.)

In 1946, Kalman Klein and David Teicholtz's Barnum Avenue Realty Corporation began construction on the 550-home Lakeville Estates. Like Levittown, the homes were initially planned for veterans returning from World War II. When the trio of three-bedroom models opened in 1951 at a cost of $12,890 to $13,990, they were advertised as "functional homes" with a recreational basement and separate bedroom area. In 1950, the developers built a large shopping plaza at the intersection of Bellmore and Merrick Avenues to serve the families who purchased these homes. This plaza would host many long-term East Meadow businesses, such as Bambi Bakery. Priced from $23,250, This is an advertisement for East Meadow Lawns, near the Wantagh Parkway. (Author's collection.)

This is an advertisement for the Suburban Gardens split-level homes in the Clearmeadow section. Several sections of Birchwood, including Birchwood Park on Newbridge Road and Birchwood at Westbury on Newbridge Avenue, were built in the vicinity. Developers noted local recreational and cultural opportunities, such as proximity to Jones Beach and Conservative synagogues, as well as the ease of commuting to New York City. (Courtesy Jeff Kraut.)

Youth sports have played an important role in the lives of children growing up in East Meadow. The East Meadow Little League, one team of which is seen above in 1955, has been offering programs for youth of all ages since the baby-boom era. The various leagues are staffed entirely by volunteers and sponsored by active local businesses. The East Meadow Soccer Club was established in 1971 and has been running continuously since that time. In 1962, legendary Brooklyn Dodgers baseball pioneer and civil rights activist Jackie Robinson visited the East Meadow High School Dads' Club meeting, as seen below. (Above, courtesy Paul Fischler; below, courtesy East Meadow UFSD No. 3.)

Eisenhower (Salisbury) Park, located north of Hempstead Turnpike, is larger than New York City's Central Park. The park features a multitude of athletic and recreational opportunities, from professional golf and aquatics to children's playgrounds. Picnics and fundraisers have been common in the park since its inception. The facility was originally designed as Nassau County Park at Salisbury and opened in 1944. Most of the land came from the foreclosed Salisbury Club, with additional parcels totaling 930 acres. The official dedication ceremonies took place in October 1949, as seen above with Gold Star Mothers and Spanish-American War Veterans viewing the parade. In October 1969, the park was rededicated as Dwight D. Eisenhower Memorial Park. The 1970 photograph below shows the Lakeside Theater on the right and the Veterans Memorial Center and Salisbury clubhouse on the left. The theater has been renamed the Harry Chapin Lakeside Theatre in memory of the singer who died on his way to a concert there in 1981. (Both, courtesy Nassau County Archives.)

The Republican Club was located just north of Newbridge Road School. Not only did it serve as the clubhouse for political events, it was also used as a local meeting hall, for religious services, and even for overflow elementary school classes. Below, Helen Hinrichs campaigns for Dwight D. Eisenhower, Edward J. Speno, and Francis C. McClosky in November 1956. Speno was a lawyer and state senator who served from 1955 until his death in 1971. His civic contributions to the East Meadow area are evidenced by the town park named for him. (Above, courtesy Gary Hammond; below, courtesy Sharon Houghey O'Gara.)

Nassau County's political machine has had a lasting impact on the way local government is run, with the Republican Party dominating political and civic organizations in East Meadow for generations. At right, John Houghey, Henry Kneuer, and local political leaders crowd around Gov. Nelson A. Rockefeller, who went on to become Gerald Ford's vice president. Below, East Meadowites catch a glimpse of Pres. Richard Nixon as he campaigns at the Nassau Coliseum. The Barnum Woods area and neighboring sections of East Meadow have traditionally aligned themselves with the Democratic Party, and gerrymandering has severed those zones from the rest of East Meadow's political scene. The local Democratic Club met at the Maple Avenue Benevolent Hall after October 1950. (Both, courtesy Sharon Houghey O'Gara.)

The St. Francis Polish National Catholic Church on Harton Avenue, seen at left, was constructed in 1932. Fr. Bernard Bobek was the first priest, and services were conducted in Polish, the first language of a number of prominent East Meadow families at that time. A Polish school was established, and Rose Gniewek organized the Women's Society in 1954. The baby-boom era brought growth to the church as well. In 1956, a new altar was constructed; a year later, a rectory was built. The Communion class of 1935 is pictured below. (Both, courtesy St. Francis Polish National Catholic Church.)

The St. Raphael Parish was founded in 1941. This Roman Catholic church was originally located on the east side of Newbridge Road at Pendroy Street. Its first priest was Fr. Charles Sullivan. Church services were held in the rectory, an old farmhouse, until the first structure was erected on the site. The first building was a small wood-frame church that was moved from East Williston in 1942. This old church is seen here during Louise and John Houghey's wedding ceremony in March 1945. The couple established their home nearby on Abington Place. (Both, courtesy Sharon Houghey O'Gara.)

St. Raphael's grew greatly under Fr. Paul Connolly as the population increased. By 1953, a new, modern church building had been constructed across the street. This brick structure, seen above in 1961, served the congregation until a larger church was built in 2004. The brick church was demolished in 2015. Below, scores of children line up at St. Raphael's Elementary School in 1961. The school served the parish until 1992. (Both, courtesy St. Raphael's Church.)

Temple Emanu-El was the first organized Jewish congregation in East Meadow. It was formed as the direct result of a catastrophic Long Island Rail Road crash on Thanksgiving Eve, November 22, 1950. On that night, 78 commuters lost their lives in the worst rail disaster on Long Island as two trains collided near Kew Gardens, Queens. One of those lost was Emanuel Frankfort of East Meadow, and mourners in the shiva house decided to form a congregation. Congregants first met in homes, in the firehouse, and in a tent. Above, this large home on Merrick Avenue, formerly of Edwin Mersereau, was purchased to serve as the congregation's first synagogue. Below, the 1955 board poses with Pres. Leon Alpern in front of the old building. (Both, courtesy Temple Emanu-El.)

Temple Emanu-El's first new synagogue was built in 1956, and its uniquely-shaped stained glass sanctuary building was constructed in 1957. The Reform congregation's first rabbi was Eugene Lipsey. Its first president was Joseph Greenberg, and first permanent cantor was Lawrence Harwood. At left, town of Hempstead presiding supervisor Thomas Gulotta and Councilman Gregory Peterson break ground on a synagogue extension with Pres. Gerald Hayden and Rabbi Bennett Herman in 1984. (Both, courtesy Temple Emanu-El.)

The East Meadow Jewish Center, a traditional Conservative congregation, was organized under Chairman George Weisbarth in July 1953. Members met in storefronts and in their homes. The first High Holiday services were held in space donated by the Republican Club on Newbridge Road, as noted in the flyer at right. Appropriately, during the dedication holiday of Chanukah in 1956, the congregation dedicated its first building. Located upstairs was a combination sanctuary/auditorium, and downstairs was a religious school wing. Growth was so rapid that by 1963, the congregation had broken ground on a large new sanctuary that increased capacity to 1,800 worshippers. Below, Rabbi Israel Nobel and Cantor Paul Carus are pictured with Rabbi Morris Schnall of the Suburban Park Jewish Center. Rabbi Nobel and Cantor Carus served the congregation for three decades, and Rabbi Ronald Androphy has been the spiritual leader since 1983. (Both, courtesy East Meadow Jewish Center.)

✡ **EAST MEADOW JEWISH CENTER**

Conservative Congregation

SERVICES

FOR THE

HIGH HOLY DAYS

ROSH HASHONAH, THURSDAY & FRIDAY, SEPT. 10, 11
YOM KIPPUR, SATURDAY · · SEPTEMBER 19

WILL BE HELD AT THE

East Meadow Republican Club
Newbridge Rd. at 8th St.
East Meadow, L. I.

FOR TICKET INFORMATION
See SIDNEY FELD, 1845 Harvey Lane

or call · ·
HE 1 - 3897
HE 7 - 8298
HE 7 - 4307
HE 1 - 0701
WA 2 - 7259w

Above, an artist's rendering from 1966 shows the outside of East Meadow Jewish Center's new sanctuary. This $400,000 wing was completed in 1964 and expanded again in 1987. The religious makeup of the Prospect Avenue and Barnum Woods sections of East Meadow was predominantly Jewish in the 1960s. At the height of the baby boom, hundreds of member families sent their children to Hebrew school at East Meadow Jewish Center. Below, this seventh grade class from 1966 numbered 85 students. (Both, courtesy East Meadow Jewish Center.)

One of the most active community service organizations in East Meadow is Kiwanis. The East Meadow Kiwanis Club was organized in April 1952 and was sponsored by the Uniondale club. Aside from bringing together community leaders through social gatherings and activities, Kiwanis has been improving lives by fundraising for children's charities, sponsoring youth groups, providing scholarships, and assisting the needy. Above, Edward Speno (left) and David Rothbaum present a flag to a member of the Boy Scouts. Below, from left to right, Dick Harken, Matt DeLac, Edward Speno, Leo Rudich, Mike Kostynick, Ed Kolbell, Joe Gelshenen, Frank Sassi, and Bill Sbrocco pose at a 1963 event. (Both, courtesy East Meadow Kiwanis.)

Kiwanians have come from all professions and religious backgrounds, representing the diversity of the community. Above, the Kiwanis Club assists Catholic convents in distributing Christmas candy in 1965. East Meadow Kiwanis has worked in partnership with the school system for decades. The club sponsors Terrific Kid awards for middle-level students who exhibit good citizenship qualities, and maintains active Key Clubs in both high schools. Below, Mike Kostynick, founding Kiwanis president, rides in the East Meadow "Jet" at a local game. The Jet is the mascot of East Meadow High School, and generations of sports fans have watched the Jet ride around the track, cheering for the home team. (Both, courtesy East Meadow Kiwanis.)

Seven

BUSINESSES AND ATTRACTIONS

The Steck household stood at the intersection of Prospect and Newbridge (now East Meadow) Avenues on property formerly owned by the Fredericks family. The old family house on the northeast corner was demolished in 1952. A farm stand operated by Jospeh "Bull" Hoeffner was erected on the southeast corner that same year. Next door, at the intersection, was the Meadow Dairy, as seen in this 1966 photograph. The business was run by Bob Rottkamp and Ernie Hatzelman. On the other side was Ed's Glass Works. (Courtesy Roseanne Hatzelman.)

One of East Meadow's earliest fast-food restaurants was Berkeley-Andrews Fortress, situated on the Lowden property at the intersection of Hempstead Turnpike (Fulton Street) and Front Street. The restaurant was constructed in 1949 and eventually became Mister Donut (later Dunkin' Donuts). In the 1982 picture below, a 1970 Firebird Formula 400 and a 1966 Ford Shelby Mustang GT350 grace the parking lot, which was frequented by students from East Meadow High School. With car culture alive and well in mid-century America, a car wash was constructed behind the building in 1957. (Above, courtesy Boston Public Library; below, courtesy Eric Hagenbruch.)

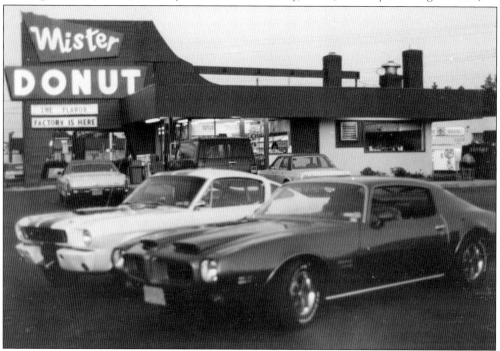

Newbridge (now East Meadow) Avenue took on the role of Main Street, with many small businesses and community services in the 1940s. Gniewek's Deli was an example of how the significant local Polish population influenced the neighborhood. The Gniewek family was instrumental in building the St. Francis Polish National Catholic Church. Raymond Gniewek went on to become the concertmaster of the Metropolitan Opera in New York City. The building pictured here became the Keyhole, then Dr. Generosity's, and finally Major's Steak House. (Both, courtesy Buczak family.)

Buczak's gas station was located at Newbridge (East Meadow) and Franklin Avenues. In 1934, Buczak's was a Texaco. It is shown here as Meadowbrook Garage in 1951. The current building dates from 1964, when it was a Shell. (Courtesy Nassau County Archives.)

One cannot speak of eating on Long Island without mentioning diners, and East Meadow has had its share! Milteades Galanes ran an older establishment called the Meadowbrook Diner (originally Meadow Brook Grill, also called "Pop's Place") until 1959 at the northeast corner of Hempstead Turnpike and Newbridge Road. The Levitt family would frequent the diner when building Levittown. In the 1950s and 1960s, mom-and-pop luncheonettes ruled in East Meadow. Schoolchildren, allowed to leave for lunch, took advantage. The Empress Diner (pictured) opened across the street in 1955 and was run from 1967 until 2018 by the Panagatos family. The Stardust Diner opened in 1966 and is now known as the Colony Diner. Finally, the Apollo Diner on Merrick Avenue began operating in 1967. Each diner was remodeled throughout the years, following fires and the latest restaurant trends. (Courtesy Panagatos family.)

116

Central Island Restaurant
Fulton Ave. & Merrick Ave.
East Hempstead, L. I., N. Y.

Restaurants appeared along Hempstead (Bethpage) Turnpike in the 1940s. This 1950 postcard shows the Central Island Restaurant. The three Borrelli brothers purchased Central Island in 1955 and converted it to an Italian restaurant, as seen below. The Borrellis, who emigrated from Naples, Italy, learned the restaurant trade in New York City and ventured out to Long Island just as the baby boom exploded in East Meadow. Business grew so quickly that large additions to the restaurant were completed in 1962. Borrelli's is still family owned and operated. (Above, courtesy Gary Hammond; below, courtesy Frank Borrelli Jr.)

Hempstead Turnpike at Merrick Ave., East Hempstead, L. I., N. Y.

Dave Shor's drive-in opened at the corner of Hempstead Turnpike and Merrick Avenue in July 1949 and quickly became a popular youth spot. Dave Shor's billed itself as "Long Island's newest, most modern drive-in restaurant," with parking for more than 500 cars. The era of the 1950s drive-in had begun, and the restaurant claimed it was "Shor" to satisfy hungry customers, serving up hamburgers, frankfurters, shakes, and other American fare. Dave Shor's added air-conditioning in 1971 and stayed in business until 1976, when the building was demolished. A bank stands on the site today. The postcard above is from 1949, and the photograph below was taken in 1959. (Above, courtesy Gary Hammond; below, courtesy Perry Julien.)

Shoe King Sam was a well-known establishment on the corner of Hempstead Turnpike and Newbridge Road. It was one of the largest discount drive-in shoe stores in the country and the leader of a small regional chain. A fire in January 1958 gutted the business and destroyed 60,000 to 70,000 pairs of shoes. Shoe King Sam's was owned by Samuel Weiss, who helped finance the first building of Temple Sholom in the Salisbury area. (Courtesy East Meadow Fire District.)

East Meadow Bowl has been a favorite attraction since 32 alleys opened in 1959. Popularity in bowling increased, and in 1962, an additional 12 alleys were installed. Since its inception, the bowling alley has hosted leagues of local organizations. It was a leader in the movement to implement computerized scoring in the 1980s. Before the bowling alley was built, the property was home to the Alsheimer Farm and then Klein's Garden Center. (Courtesy Sharon Houghey O'Gara.)

The Levittown Roller Rink operated from 1955 to 1986 on the north side of Hempstead Turnpike, just west of the Meadowbrook Parkway. While many youngsters came to the rink to enjoy themselves with their friends, it was also a major producer of national skating champions. The rink was owned by the America on Wheels chain. Levittown Roller Rink was popular with children, teens, and adults right through its closing. The building became the discount drugstore Rockbottom, which also opened in the Lakeville Estates shopping center on Bellmore Avenue, next to Nassau Kosher Meats. (Both, courtesy Eric S. Poliak.)

"Make A Date To Roller Skate"

LEVITTOWN ROLLER RINK

Hempstead Tpke. & Wantagh Parkway
East Meadow, L. I., N. Y.
PErshing 1-6200

Sessions: Nightly 7:30 PM to 11:00 PM
Every evening excepting Mondays
Matinees: Saturdays, Sundays & Holidays
2:00 to 5:00 PM
Special rates for: Groups, Churches & Organizations

COMING UP—TWO EXCITING ROLLER SKATING PARTIES
"Valentine's Day Party"—Wednesday, February 15, 1961
Prizes: Beautiful Plush Dolls & Animals
"Barnskate Party"—Thursday, March 2, 1961
Prizes: Transistor Radio
SKATE TILL MIDNIGHT—BOTH PARTIES

Anyone who grew up in baby-boom East Meadow remembers the Kitchen Sink sundae at Jahn's, an old-fashioned ice cream parlor on Hempstead Turnpike. It was part of a small chain started by John Jahn in 1897 that expanded across New York City and Long Island. After Jahn's, Friendly's became the popular ice cream spot. East Meadow had two Friendly's, one on Front Street and the other on Hempstead Turnpike. The Meadowbrook Theatre near Jahn's opened in 1949 as a large Art Deco auditorium with a balcony. (Courtesy Eric S. Poliak.)

In the Mitchel Manor Shopping Plaza, Food Fair (pictured under demolition in 1979) was replaced by Waldbaum's Supermarket, previously located at Merrick and Bellmore Avenues. On both sides of Food Fair was a strip mall that featured long-lasting East Meadow businesses such as Brodie's Kosher Delicatessen, MAB Liquors, Rose's Pizza, National Shoes, Pell Bakery, Liggett Drugs, and Woolworth's. The luncheonette on the corner was very popular with local youths. (Courtesy Christopher Smith.)

THE **ROOSEVELT**

Long Island's "Dream" **MOTEL - HOTEL**

A dichotomous relationship existed between the Roosevelt Motel and the Salisbury Club, seen here in 1961. The Roosevelt billed itself as Long Island's "dream" motel-hotel but focused mainly on discount lodging, while across the street in Salisbury (Eisenhower) Park sat an old clubhouse-turned-restaurant that catered to a more exclusive clientele. Today, the Salisbury Clubhouse is the Carltun, a privately run restaurant and catering hall. The Roosevelt Hotel still exists as a discount motel. (Both, courtesy Gary Hammond.)

If you missed last Sunday's
"After the beach party" at penrods...

There's another one this sunday, from 7p.m. on!
(photo taken last sunday at penrods)

Penrod's, which operated under Marty Ross and Jerry Worth, then Dan Bracciodieta from 1974 to 1977, was the first major dance club on Long Island during the height of the disco craze. Its subterranean dance floor attracted "sophisticated, fun-loving" young people who wanted to enjoy a night out to records spun by disc jockey Jackie McCloy. Penrod's eventually became Zachary's Nightclub under owner Rennie Leone. Modell's was located in the same shopping plaza, owned by the Weiss family, who operated large greenhouses on the property. Modell's, seen below in 1962, was a fixture in East Meadow for decades, selling sporting goods and, for several years, discount retail items. (Above, courtesy Jackie McCloy; below, courtesy Kathleen Botsfod.)

Once the baby boom began, East Meadow lost its downtown feel, and local residents flocked to Hempstead Turnpike for their shopping needs. In the 1960s and 1970s, "cruising the Turnpike" was a common activity. In nearby Levittown, May's was the largest local department store, seen above at a 10th anniversary celebration in 1957. William Levitt built this shopping area when his Levittown was initially laid out. F.W. Woolworth's was located in the same plaza, as seen below in 1957. May's became Tri-County Flea Market, host of the Long Island Jewelry Exchange. (Above, courtesy Levittown Public Library; below, courtesy Library of Congress.)

Here is a 1967 view of the Hempstead Turnpike in Levittown. It is hard to imagine that just a few years before this photograph was taken, potato fields and farmhouses dominated the same landscape. The quick success of Levittown enabled the developers to build a similar community in Pennsylvania, near Trenton, New Jersey. (Courtesy Levittown Public Library.)

The Crystalbrook catering hall was originally Seligman's farmhouse and then Savini's Catering Hall, run by Danny Savini. Located at the corner of Adelaide Court and Newbridge (East Meadow) Avenue, the bright entrance welcomed partygoers. This photograph was taken in 1988; the catering hall was knocked down a decade later to make way for a strip mall. (Courtesy Nassau County Archives.)

Goldblatt's Sand Pit of the East Hempstead Sand and Gravel Company became a popular hangout spot for the neighborhood's teenagers during the baby-boom era. Goldblatt ran into trouble in 1958 when the Town of Hempstead attempted to rezone the property, which he had been mining since 1927, to prevent disruption to the water table. A lawsuit against the town's decision reached the US Supreme Court in 1962. Justice Tom C. Clark argued that the ordinance was constitutional even if it deprived Goldblatt of his property or the ability to run his business. The sandpit, which would frequently flood, caused accidents and injuries to mischievous youngsters. Today, the remnants of the pit have been incorporated into a storm basin north of Speno Park. (Courtesy Hoeffner family.)

Pat Lordi's, located at the northwest corner of Hempstead Turnpike and Newbridge Road, was a family fun park that had a miniature golf course and driving range. Children of the 1950s fondly remember the trampoline park at Lordi's, which was a reflection of an American fitness and recreation fad of the decade. Men, women, and children alike would pay by the hour to practice their acrobatic feats at Jumpsville USA. The owner Pascal Lordi later operated the golf pro shop in Eisenhower Park and served as president of the East Meadow Chamber of Commerce. (Author's collection.)

BIBLIOGRAPHY

Clarke, Mary Louise. *East Meadow: Its History, Our Heritage.* East Meadow, NY: 1952.

Crosby, Alexander L. *1955: The Year We Opened Six Schools.* East Meadow, NY: East Meadow School District, 1955.

Divan, Marge. Interview by Scott Eckers. March 16, 2016.

East Meadow Public Library. *East Meadow: Its Past and Present, 1858–1976.* East Meadow, NY: East Meadow Public Library, 1976.

Hoeffner, Raymond. Interview by Scott Eckers. January 31, 2016.

Huenke, Art. *Arrt's Archives: Your Online Museum of the Long Island Rail Road and Gallery of Railroad Photos.* www.arrts-arrchives.com/. Accessed January 30, 2016.

Krahn, Frederick A. *A History of the East Meadow Public Library.* East Meadow, NY: East Meadow Public Library, 1995.

Kroplick, Howard. *Vanderbilt Cup Races.* www.vanderbiltcupraces.com.

Lemle, Zach. *Old Long Island: Brookholt.* www.oldlongisland.com/2009/11/brookholt.html. Accessed January 30, 2016.

Oberle, Joan. Interview by Scott Eckers. February 7, 2016.

Spinzia, Judith and Raymond. *Long Island's Prominent Families in the Town of Hempstead: Their Estates and Country Homes.* College Station, TX: VirtualBookworm, 2010.

Swopes, Bryan R. *This Day in Aviation: Important Dates in Aviation History.* www.thisdayinaviation.com /11-february-1939/. Accessed March 21, 2016.

Other sources include various articles from the *Brooklyn Daily Eagle, Freeport Daily Review, Long Island Daily Press, Long Island Herald, Nassau Daily Review-Star, New York Times, Newsday, Queens County Sentinel,* and *Hempstead Sentinel,* as well as archives and records of the East Meadow Fire District, East Meadow Union Free School District No. 3, Nassau County, Town of Hempstead, United Methodist Church, and Wenwood Oaks Civic Association.

For more information, please visit www.eastmeadowhistory.org, the companion site for this book.

Discover Thousands of Local History Books
Featuring Millions of Vintage Images

Arcadia Publishing, the leading local history publisher in the United States, is committed to making history accessible and meaningful through publishing books that celebrate and preserve the heritage of America's people and places.

Find more books like this at
www.arcadiapublishing.com

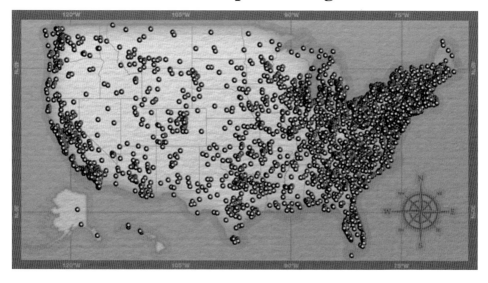

Search for your hometown history, your old stomping grounds, and even your favorite sports team.

Consistent with our mission to preserve history on a local level, this book was printed in South Carolina on American-made paper and manufactured entirely in the United States. Products carrying the accredited Forest Stewardship Council (FSC) label are printed on 100 percent FSC-certified paper.